Unearthing the Past

Unearthing the Past
Douglas Palmer, Joyce Tyldesley, and Paul Bahn

First published in Great Britain in 2005
by Mitchell Beazley, an imprint of
Octopus Publishing Group Ltd
2–4 Heron Quays, London E14 4JP

ISBN 1 84000 989 6

A CIP record for this book is available from the
British Library

Set in Berthold Akzidenz Grotesk and Minion

Colour reproduction by Bright Arts, Hong Kong
Printed and bound in China by Toppan

Commissioning Editor Vivien Antwi
Executive Art Editor Yasia Williams-Leedham
Senior Editor Peter Taylor
Design Grade Design Consultants, London
Production Gary Hayes
Copy-editor Henry Russell
Proofreader Siobhan O'Connor
Indexer Sue Farr

MITCHELL BEAZLEY

Douglas Palmer
Paul Bahn
Joyce Tyldesley

Unearthing the Past

The great discoveries of archaeology from around the world

INTRODUCTION

To discover where we have come from, how we got here, and how our ancestors lived and died is part of our uniquely human desire to find and place ourselves in the world today. Henry Ford may not have liked it but our human past provides a neverending source of interest, fascination, and excitement. Exploration of that past can be revelatory and deeply satisfying, whether simply reading about it, visiting some famous site such as Pompeii in Italy or the Great Pyramids of Egypt, or becoming directly involved with the search for information and understanding about the past. I have personal experience of how the evidence of archaeology can affect lives. My wife and I took two giggly young girls to see the Magdalenian cave paintings at Lascaux in France. The short descent underground through the rock walled passage and into the cave subdued them. But it was the overwhelming power of the amazing images of the animals of the ice ages that literally dumbfounded them even though they knew the cave they were visiting and paintings they were seeing are replicas of the 15,000-year-old originals.

Unearthing the Past explores a selection of the most important and interesting discoveries which the pursuit and discipline of archaeology have uncovered around the world over the last few centuries. The diversity of subject matter and the huge range of topics which come under the very wide "umbrella" of modern archaeology can only be touched upon. We have chosen seven main themes to illustrate the wonderful scope of archaeological investigation. From our initial glimpse at "Our Prehistoric Ancestors", we search through ancient "Tombs and Burial Sites", and hear about some of the fabulous "Cities and Dwelling Places" of the past before considering the "Art, Intellect, and Religion" of our ancestors which remind us that our human capacity for thought and inspiration have not changed. Then we face up to the salutary evidence for neverending "War and Human Conflict'" and the all too familiar human needs for "Migration and Colonization" and their

associated problems. Finally, there is a section on "Science and Archaeology" which introduces just some of the new interdisciplinary methodology and techniques from science which have helped transform archaeology in recent decades. For example the various techniques of dating have helped revolutionize the chronology of our human ancestors and relatives and debunk some of the mythology surrounding forgeries such as the Turin Shroud and the Piltdown Man.

The very definition of archaeology as a discipline has radically changed over the last century or so. In the past the subject was first dominated by the study of antiquities with an emphasis on the Classical and Biblical worlds, then with prehistoric times, finding traces of the peoples of those times from their bones, buildings and burials and any associated materials such as pottery, tools, and weaponry.

Now the field of archaeology has greatly broadened and deepened to include the study of the past in general through the recovery and analysis of the physical remains of human related materials and traces of human activities, even if they are less than 100 years old. The pursuit of archaeology aims to recover and describe the material remains of past humans and their activities. In so doing it enables us to reconstruct the structure and behaviour of these past societies and understand the reasons for their activities.

All around the world important new discoveries about prehistory and ancient history are being made every week. Some of the discoveries instantly make headline news around the world such as the 7 million year old skeletal remains of Sahelanthropus tchadensis, nicknamed Toumai, from Chad in Africa. Others take years to filter through the archaeological "grapevine" and then are only reported in academic journals but such is the global nature of modern communications that most really important finds soon become widely known. A number of popular archaeology magazines, and television programs help to highlight new information and discoveries.

Some finds, like the Toumai one, are the fruition of years of patient searching, often in very inhospitable environments like the Sub-Saharan desert sands of Chad. Other finds, like the sculpted stone remains of a 1,200 year-old city near the famous 7th century Mahablipuram temple on India's south coast and the Neolithic wooden structure on Holme beach in Norfolk, England, are the result of "accidental" natural processes. Both are ancient manmade structures that have been submerged over the centuries by rising sealevels and covered with recent sediment deposits. The Indian remains are probably part of extensive submerged ruins that have been mapped by marine archaeologists over the last few years. Their present "resurrection" and exposure are due to the drastic scouring action of the last year's devastating tsunamis in the Indian Ocean. The Norfolk structure was also brought to light when winter storms from the North Sea swept away the sand that had been protecting them.

These days, many of the revelatory "nuggets" about our distant past are made in archaeological laboratories with sophisticated equipment operated by highly trained and skilled professionals. For instance, recent 3D computed tomographic (CAT) scans of King Tutankhamun's skull show no sign of the murderous and fatal blow to his head which had been suspected because of previous x-rays. Those revealed two bone fragments which seemed to have come from a skull fracture. But the new more detailed scans indicate that the fragments do not belong to the skull and were probably introduced accidentally by the original embalmers over three thousand years ago or by Howard Carter's team who discovered the mummy in 1922.

The same kind of scans plus sophisticated computer modeling techniques have also been used to reconstruct Toumai's skull and face. The original skull was somewhat deformed by geological processes and this fuelled arguments over whether it was more or less ape-like in its form. The computer graphic remodeling has allowed the distortion to be removed and the resulting skull form seems to be less ape-like than its critics claimed. And, from the remodeled skull an interpretation of the original face has been reconstructed.

But many finds, including some of the most important are still made in the field by both trained and amateur archaeologists driven by the common passion to know more and about our past and understand more about our ancestors. One of the most spectacular of recent finds is that of the diminutive skeletal remains of a new human relative Homo floresiensis, from a limestone cave on the Indonesian island of Flores. The discovery raises many fascinating questions such as the whole definition of our genus and the brainsize related to it. Such finds which claim major changes to past perceptions tend to be hotly disputed and the Flores find has been no exception with some critics saying that it is no more than a microcephalic modern human. Again CT scanning has helped resolve the issue showing that the form of its brain is much closer to that of Homo erectus than a microcephalic modern human.

At the same time as all these wonderful discoveries which advance our knowledge and understanding there are also sad losses of our global human heritage. Unfortunately, the plunder of graves and burial sites is a very ancient human trait and it is an ongoing one which today feeds an international trade in the extraordinary and often very beautiful objects made by long forgotten craftspeople. Repeatedly, important and irreplaceable sites are damaged or destroyed sometimes in the name of progress and development, sometimes by natural processes and sometimes by wanton acts of destruction associated with conflict such as the giant Buddha carvings in Afghanistan blown up by the Taliban. Maybe the archaeological study of conflict will eventually help us to understand its causes.

1

OUR PREHISTORIC ANCESTORS

Over the past 6 or 7 million years, since we last shared a common ancestor with the chimps, many species of human relatives have evolved. All but one have died out, leaving us, *Homo sapiens*, the most globalized and dominant primate. It is only within the past 200 years that we have finally come to know and understand something of our own story. Here we highlight just a few of the remarkable finds of that prehistory from the 3.7-million-year-old footprints from Laetoli in Africa to the astonishingly well-preserved body of Ötzi, the Neolithic "Ice Man" from the Tyrolean Alps.

The desire to trace our ancestry ranges from the current boom in family history to the more academic pursuit of our most ancient and extinct fossil human relatives. While historical information is hidden away in dusty archives and record offices, the prehistoric data is locked away in the equally dusty rock record of ancient sediments, often in remote corners of the world. Our interest and concern here is with the latter prehistoric record of human ancestry which is now known to date back some 7 million years.

It is only some 200 years since most scientists still believed in the special creation of humanity within the past few thousand years. In the mid 19th century Charles Darwin felt so apprehensive about the application of his theory of evolution to humans that he confined his comments in *The Origin of Species* to suggesting "that light would be shed on the ancestry of man". Even that apparently innocuous comment was enough to evoke severe criticism. Not until the end of the 19th century was there any general acceptance of Darwin's contention that we do share a common ancestor with the higher apes – an ancestor who also lived in Africa.

This African ancestry has now been amply verified by the fossil evidence of bones and stones and recent biomolecular genetic studies. Thanks to recent discoveries, there are now three ancient fossil relatives over 4 million years old – *Ardipithecus ramidus*, *Orrorin tugenensis* and *Sahelanthropus tchadensis*. And of these the latter is some 7 million years old, dating from a time when our last shared ancestor with the chimps lived. However, as we shall see, there are also some interesting complexities in the story of how our ancestors expanded beyond Africa. Here we can only investigate a small sample of our fascinating family history and the family tree which at present includes some 20 separate human-related species, of which all but one – our own species *Homo sapiens* – are now extinct. Very few of the original find spots for these ancient relatives can be visited, but we have selected some such as Olduvai Gorge (see Laetoli, Tanzania) and the Neanderthal site of

Feldhofer Grotto in Germany. However, the fossil finds (or replicas of them) from other sites are sometimes to be seen in museums. For example, the remarkable frozen cadaver of "Ötzi", the Neolithic man found in mountain glacial ice near the Italian/Austrian border, can be viewed in the South Tyrol Museum of Archaeology in Bolzano, Italy.

Although the African ancestry of our species may date back some 200,000 years or more, we still know very little about that early African phase. Nevertheless, new discoveries have uncovered Ethiopian fossil remains of our species dating back to around 195,000 years ago. But the bulk of our information comes from much more recent finds postdating the "diaspora" out of Africa, and the Ice Ages, which devastated high latitudes until some 15,000 years ago.

Members of our species reached the Middle East by around 90,000 years ago, where they may well have first encountered the encumbent Neanderthal people. Within another 40,000 years, humans reached as far as Australia (perhaps as early as 60,000 years ago). Early penetration into more northern climes was prevented by the frequency of glacial conditions, but around 15,000 years ago we have spectacular evidence from Mezhirich in Ukraine of human adaptation to the cold weather. At the end of the last Ice Age, and on the other side of the world, Monte Verde in Chile records the earliest well-documented site of human settlement in the Americas, followed by the Clovis sites from the USA.

Finally, Ötzi, the 5200-year-old Tyrolean "Ice Man", brings us close to historic times. Our discussion of the find illustrates how modern investigative techniques can provide a wealth of often surprising information. The exceptional preservation of Ötzi's body and his possessions due to the freeze-drying processes of burial in ice combined with the use of number of scientific disciplines – from palaeobotany to forensic science – give us an astonishing insight into the life and times of this Neolithic hunter.

FOOTPRINTS IN THE ROCK
Laetoli, Tanzania

The remarkable discovery of fossil footprints nearly 4 million years old helped to overthrow old ideas about human evolution.

Charles Darwin predicted that the origin of humankind was to be found in Africa; after all, he argued, that is where our nearest living relatives, the chimpanzees and gorillas, live. More than a century of searching has uncovered a wealth of fossil evidence which proves that he was right. We now have a human family tree comprising more than 20 different species of human-linked ancestors and relatives who have lived and died out over the past 7 million years, mainly in Africa. Modern genetic techniques have shown that all living humans are remarkably closely related and share a common African ancestry dating back around 120,000 years.

Finding connections
By the first decades of the 20th century, the existence of extinct human relatives such as the Eurasian Neanderthals and the Asian *Homo erectus* people was no longer in doubt. But our deeper fossil ancestry and the link to the ancestors we share with the higher apes were still unknown. Darwin's claim of our African ancestry had yet to be proved. There were fundamental and unanswered questions about how and when human evolution had occurred. The general view was that our closest human relatives had large brains, walked upright, and had somehow "sprung" from much more primitive and small-brained, ape-like ancestors who moved on all fours and did not make tools or have any culture.

By the 1950s numerous fossil discoveries confirmed that our deep ancestry was indeed African. Raymond Dart and Robert Broom found some very ape-like fossils, named *Australopithecus* ("southern ape"), in South Africa, and claimed that they were part of human ancestry. Similar fossils were later discovered further north at Olduvai by Louis and Mary Leakey (see box).

With more and more investigators being attracted to Africa, the search intensified for the elusive "link" between such ape-like remains and the more human-like *Homo erectus*. One of the most fascinating questions was which human characteristics emerged first: large brains, upright walking, or tool-making? Perhaps they had all happened at once. Then the Leakeys found a new fossil relative, which Louis named *Homo habilis*, meaning "handyman", because he thought it manufactured the primitive stone tools found at Olduvai. But when did upright walking first develop? Dart had claimed that his little *Australopithecus africanus* moved in this way, but not many experts agreed with him.

A lucky find
The dramatic discovery which confirmed Dart's view and overthrew many previous ideas about human evolution was made in the 1970s, when some very human-looking footprints dating from about 3.7 million years ago were found at Laetoli in Tanzania.

In 1976 some of Mary Leakey's co-workers were amusing themselves by playing "African

Key Facts: Laetoli

Location: Tanzania	**Explored by:** Mary Leakey's field team, which included Paul Abell
Age: 3.7 million years	
Discovered: First tracks 1976; Australopithecine footprints found by Paul Abell in 1979	**Display:** Cast on display in nearby Olduvai Gorge Museum

Louis and Mary Leakey

Olduvai Gorge, near the Ngoro Ngoro Crater in Tanzania, was the first prehistoric site in Africa to be explored in detail. The excavations there were carried out from 1937 by Louis Leakey (1903–72) and his second wife, Mary (1913–96), palaeoanthropologists in search of human-related bones and stone tools as evidence for the African ancestry of humankind.

In many ways a maverick, Louis Leakey had little rigorous scientific training. His research was expensive, and most of his finance came from sponsors. Having raised the money, he felt under pressure to deliver results, and that may have been why he sometimes got carried away and made extravagant claims that have not stood up to close scrutiny.

The dry ravines of Olduvai gorge expose horizontal layers of sedimentary deposits, the most recent at the top and progressively older layers beneath. The first important find consisted of crude stone tools in the oldest layers (Bed 1 and the lower part of Bed 2), which cross the boundary between the Pliocene and the Pleistocene around 1.8 million years ago. By far the oldest and most primitive stone tools known at the time of their discovery, they are part of the Oldowan culture. Since then, tools have been discovered in Ethiopia that date back to 2.6 million years ago.

Despite the importance of Leakey's discovery, he was frustrated by his failure to find any associated bones that might have given some clue to the kind of beings that had made the Olduvai tools. But finally, in 1959, after nearly 30 years' work, Mary Leakey found the spectacular skull of a robust Australopithecine which Louis named *Zinjanthropus boisei* and is now known as *Paranthropus boisei*. Yet even that was not really what the Leakeys had been looking for: the clinching discovery came a decade later, when Mary found *Homo habilis*, the "handyman" which Louis claimed was the so-called "missing link" between extinct ape-like species and the earliest, now extinct species of human.

snowballs", throwing elephant dung at each other, when they noticed some footprints. On further investigation these turned out to lie on a trackway which had evidently been used by a variety of animals – 20 in all – including elephant, buffalo, giraffe, and antelope. There were also tiny, delicate bird prints, and patterns caused by raindrops. The impressions had all originally been made on the soft surface of a fresh fall of ash emitted from the Sadiman volcano some 20 km (12 miles) away. After the animals had passed over the deposit, it cooled and hardened into rock, which was later buried by further ashfalls and riverbed sediment.

Mary Leakey realized at once that if the prints of animals had been preserved, there was an outside chance that those of human-related species might also be present. But it was not until July 1979 that Paul Abell, a geochemist, spotted what looked like a new set of tracks. Ndibo Mbuika, one of Mary's most experienced excavators, was sent to investigate and confirmed that they had indeed found two sets of very human-like prints side by side. The larger pair had a curious "double-strike" imprint, which was finally interpreted as having been made by a third individual stepping in the tracks of the larger of his or her companions.

A walk set in stone

When finally excavated, the double trackway was found to extend for 23 m (75 ft). It contained 47 large and 27 small footprints. The volcanic ash that preserved these traces included tiny crystals

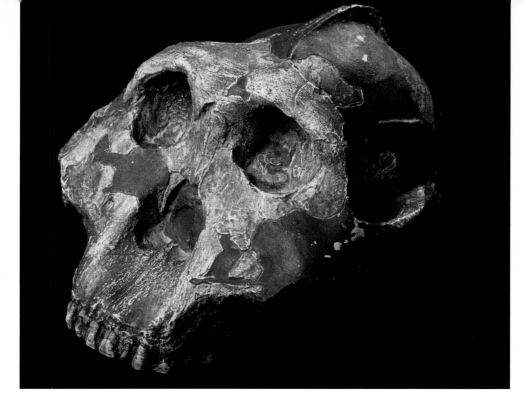

Left: A partly restored skull of a so-called "robust" Australopithecine – *Paranthropus boisei*, nicknamed "nutcracker man" by Louis Leakey, whose team found the first skull at Olduvai in 1959. The massive bone structure strengthens the skull for the stresses of eating tough plant material.

of minerals that were formed in lava and which contain chemical elements that have radioisotopes of the kind that can be dated (see radiometric dating, p. 166). Tests showed that the ash had been deposited approximately 3.6 million years ago.

Mary Leakey described the prints as "the most remarkable find I have made in my entire career". All the scientists involved in the discovery were amazed to see such clear evidence that our ancient relatives had walked upright. The people who had left these traces were simply too old to be members of our own genus *Homo*. So which human relative had made the tracks? As no skeleton was found at the end of the path, it was impossible to tell.

During the mid 1970s, there were numerous new fossil finds in other parts of Africa, one of which revealed a previously unknown human-related species, which was named *Australopithecus afarensis*, but was known informally by its discoverer, American palaeoanthropologist Don Johanson, as Lucy. Excavated in 1974 at Hadar in Ethiopia, Lucy had lived some 3.8 million years ago, and was thus significantly older than Raymond Dart's discovery. Analysis of Lucy's knee bones suggested that she had been capable of bipedal (upright) walking.

It was not long before the Laetoli discovery was romanticized into a Pliocene lovers' lane down which the two Australopithecines – who were taken to be a male and a female – walked calmly arm in arm away from the volcanic eruption, while behind them a child stepped in the footprints of the male. A nice story, but one for which there is no hard scientific evidence.

Preservation

Laetoli lies in a remote part of the Ngoro Ngoro Crater Conservation Area. Although it was originally hoped that the prehistoric site could be preserved under the cover of a building and opened to the general public, that proved impractical. In 1991 the Antiquities Department of the Tanzanian government obtained funds from the Getty Conservation Unit in the USA to assess the future risks to the tracks and how best to preserve them. In August 1996 the footprints were carefully reburied. The site is now maintained and guarded by the local Masai community. Four months after the ceremonial reburial Mary Leakey died. A replica of the tracks is now displayed at the small Olduvai Museum that overlooks the gorge near the Ngoro Ngoro Crater and the Serengeti Game Park.

A PREHISTORIC BUTCHERY
Boxgrove, England

Finds at the butchery site of Boxgrove have shed new light on the world of early humans in Europe half a million years ago.

In the early 1980s, commercial quarrying activity at Boxgrove in West Sussex revealed underlying prehistoric material more or less intact. Investigated by Mark Roberts between 1982 and 1986, Boxgrove is a butchery site at the foot of what was once a huge chalk cliff. It is about half a million years old. Until it was discovered, archaeologists believed that Britain was first occupied somewhat more recently than that. The Boxgrove people probably lived in the forested downland above the cliff, which then stood on the edge of a shallow sea. Animals wandered around the lagoons and beaches below them.

Boxgrove is not a single site, but preserves a series of isolated activities on different land surfaces spanning tens of thousands of years and occupying a range of environments from coastal/marine to open grassland and cold tundra. These land surfaces are among the best preserved Lower Palaeolithic specimens in the world.

A handaxe factory

There are thousands of stone tools at Boxgrove, including hundreds of handaxes. They have been preserved in perfect condition because they were covered with silt from the tide rising on the coastal mudflats.

The site seems to have been the floor of a handaxe factory. The flint flakes there lay undisturbed until the late 20th century from the time they were freshly worked and discarded by the ancient craftsmen. These fragments and the tools have now been pieced together to show, in the most detailed way, exactly how the handaxes were made. The people who lived here obtained flint from collapsed cliffs and screes. Large numbers of flint nodules were used as anvils, while beach pebbles were employed as hammerstones to smash animal bones open in order to obtain their edible marrow.

Experts used modern replicas of the handaxes to cut up deer and sheep, and skin their carcasses. The tools proved highly efficient at both tasks. Many of the original weapons show signs of wear which could probably only have been caused by butchering meat.

Rhino hunters

Until the discovery of the Boxgrove site, it was fashionable to believe that ancient people were mainly scavengers, but the Sussex find indicates that they were hunters. For example, circular perforations on a horse's shoulder blade are thought to be spear wounds, while butchery marks show that the animals were intact when they were captured – the cut marks always underlie or precede gnaw marks, where these occur, which means that wild animals did not have access to the meat until the humans had finished with it.

The freshly killed animals were cut up with soft tissue such as tongue and eyeballs still in place; scavengers do not normally have use of such parts because they have previously been taken by birds and other predators. In addition, some of the butchered animals, particularly the

Key Facts: Boxgrove	
Location: West Sussex, England	excavated here from 1982–6, and again in the mid 1990s
Date: Lower Palaeolithic, 500,000 years	
Discovered: Artefacts first found in the early 1970s	**Display:** Artefacts housed in the British Museum, bones in the Natural History Museum
Explored by: British archaeologist Mark Roberts, who	

Above: A view of the
excavations at Boxgrove in
the mid 1990s, showing the
series of trenches separated
by metre-wide baulks.

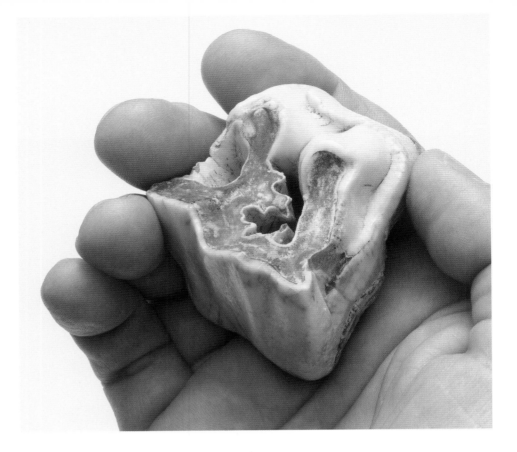

mature rhinoceroses, had no natural predators among the carnivores known to have existed at Boxgrove – one section alone contained the remains of four rhinos, each skilfully cut up and filleted, with bones smashed for the marrow.

The theory that these early humans were hunters is further supported by a discovery at Schöningen, Germany. Archaeologist found three carefully constructed wooden spears, each about 2 m (3.56 ft) long, which dated from between 350,000 and 400,000 years ago.

One horse at Boxgrove was taken apart in at least seven stages, the flint tools being renewed at the start of each phase. It seems that the marrow and the soft tissue (such as liver) were eaten at the site of the kill, and that only the muscle blocks and skin were transported away. At least eight people sat in a circle around the horse carcass, making the stone tools with which to butcher it. This is shown by the piles of flint chippings they left behind: the eight distinctive piles formed characteristic triangular shapes, made as the hunters knelt on the ground with flakes falling between their legs in front of them.

Human remains

In 1993 a gnawed human tibia (shinbone) was discovered at Boxgrove, followed in 1995 by two large, well-worn human teeth. These are the oldest human fragments ever found in Britain. They suggested that the hominid to whom they belonged was robust and heavily muscled, about 1.82 m (6 ft) tall and weighing 83 kg (182 lb). Archaeologists have identified him as *Homo heidelbergensis*, an ancestor of modern Europeans. The teeth had clearly been used as tools or grips, which increased the wear on them. They had serious build-up of plaque from bacteria, and showed the onset of periodontal disease. Scratch marks on the front of the teeth had been made by flints – Boxgrove man had evidently been in the habit of holding a lump of meat in his left hand, gripping it with his teeth, then sawing off pieces with a stone tool, using his teeth as a vice-cum-cutting board – and the fact that the scratches went from top left to bottom right indicated that he was right-handed.

It has not so far been possible to assign any seasonality to Boxgrove activities because so many

Dmanisi

Dmanisi is a medieval town in the Republic of Georgia, which once overlooked the old Silk Road through the Caucasus region. Beneath its ruins a team led by David Lordkipanidze has unearthed some of the oldest human remains outside Africa, dating to about 1.77 million years ago, a period when the site was located on a peninsula between the Black and Caspian seas, along a land corridor into Eurasia.

Since 1991, bones from as many as six individuals have been recovered from the same layer, including four skulls, one of which is particularly well preserved and complete. They seem to belong to the same species, although they range in size from enormous (one jawbone is markedly bigger than the rest) to relatively small.

These specimens had tiny brains – less than half as large as those of modern humans – with huge canine teeth, a small nose, and thin brow ridges, which all look too ape-like for an advanced hominid capable of migrating into a new continent.

Reconstructions of the faces produce results that look far more primitive than *Homo erectus*, and rather resemble *Homo habilis*. This has led some specialists to suggest that the specimens should be dubbed *Homo georgicus*.

One skull and jawbone from the site had lost all but one tooth several years before death at well over 40, so this individual had clearly survived for a long time without eating food that required heavy chewing – perhaps by consuming soft plant and animal foods, or with the help of other people, which raises interesting questions about social structure at this time.

Thousands of simple stone tools (including choppers and scrapers) have emerged from the same sediments, as have hundreds of animal bones. Among the latter are the remains of wolves, the extinct giant deer, and sabre-toothed cats; the latter's fangs are a perfect fit for holes in one of the human skulls.

of the bones are very fragmentary; however, as it is known that the climate in this period was similar to today's, and that the animals would therefore not have needed to move off in the winter, it can be assumed that the site was occupied year-round. With or without fire – and to date no trace of it has been found there – the inhabitants would certainly have needed rudimentary clothing to survive an English winter.

Enormous quantities of meat were obtained at Boxgrove: a single rhinoceros could have yielded up to 700 kg (1543 lb) of edible food; a large horse 400 kg (882 lb). The meticulous butchery carried out indicates that all the meat was removed and required, and the huge quantities imply either large groups of people or that the meat was treated and stored for later use, which in turn suggests food sharing, future planning, and perhaps even a need for language.

In recent years, more evidence has come to light – for example, from the coast of East Anglia – that people were in Britain even before Boxgrove was occupied. One site with stone tools may be as old as 700,000 years old.

OUR NEANDERTHAL COUSINS
Feldhofer Grotto, Germany

For 10,000 years, modern humans in Europe coexisted with another related species, the Neanderthals, who had robust, stocky bodies adapted to cold conditions.

Historically, the first species to be recognized as related to but different from modern humans (*Homo sapiens*) is Neanderthal man (*Homo neanderthalis*). Neanderthal remains were first found in Germany in the mid 19th century, but it still took decades for scientists to confirm the link between them and humans.

The main problem was one of acceptance: how could these people, who were generally described as "nasty, brutish, and short", be our relatives? There is evidence that Neanderthals coexisted with early humans in Europe, perhaps for as long as 10,000 years, but what was the nature of their interaction? The recovery of DNA showed that Neanderthals were not the ancestors of modern humans of Eurasian origin. This discovery raised the question of how Neanderthals, who had survived the vicissitudes of Ice Age climates for at least 300,000 years, came to be replaced by migrants from Africa.

Acknowledging a relative

In the early decades of the 19th century, numerous finds of stone tools and even buried human skeletons associated with Ice Age animals were made across Europe. But such was the power of the prevailing mind-set that it was many years before people acknowledged the idea of human prehistory. One of the most important finds was made in 1856 in the Feldhofer Grotto, a limestone cave in the valley of the Neander River near Dusseldorf. A variety of bones and stone tools were dug out of deposits on a cave floor by

quarrymen who were excavating the limestone rock to make lime. They took their discoveries to a local schoolmaster, Johann Fuhlrott, who noted a strong similarity between some of the skeletal remains and recently published illustrations of a gorilla's skeleton. The skull bones had a prominent eyebrow ridge and lacked the forehead that typifies the modern human.

Fuhlrott and Hermann Schaaffhausen, a professor of anatomy, published an accurate description of the find with illustrations, but they baulked at drawing the obvious conclusion – that they had discovered a new species of related human being. Instead, they meekly suggested that the bones belonged to a member of a savage race that may have coexisted with the animals whose bones were also found there. Yet even these modest claims were greeted with scepticism. The break-through eventually came in 1864 when William King, a professor of palaeontology in Galway, Ireland, described the bones from the Neander valley as those of a human-related species. It was he who coined the term *Homo neanderthalis*.

Hunters of the Ice Age

Today we know that the Neanderthals were a remarkably successful human-related species who lived for more than 300,000 years, until 28,000 years ago when they finally died out. They occupied a huge territory that extended from North Wales to the Caucasus, and from Gibraltar to Palestine. They were tough hunters who were well adapted to the fluctuating and often harsh

---

Key Facts: Feldhofer Grotto

Location: Neander Valley, Germany

Age: 40,000 years

Discovered: 1856 by local quarrymen

Explored by: Johann Fuhlrott and Hermann Schaaffhausen

Display: Neanderthal Museum, Mettmann, Germany

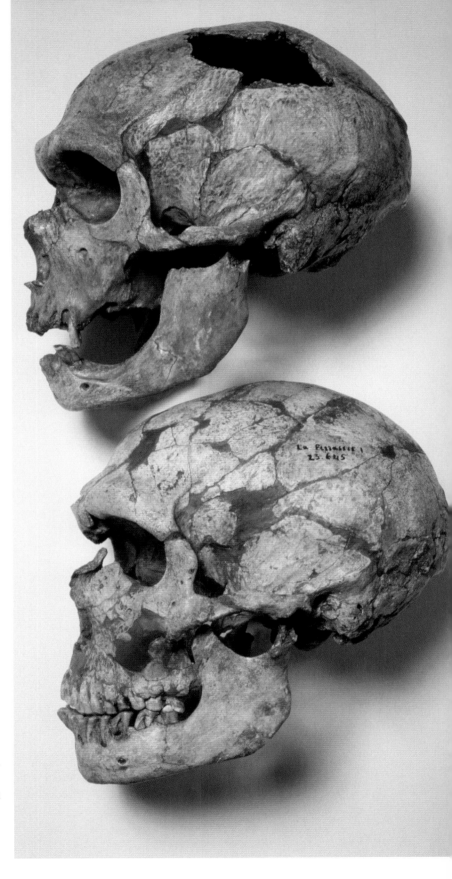

Right: **The discovery of fairly complete Neanderthal skulls at La Ferrassie in France led to a better understanding of their anatomy, but with some misinterpretation because of the use of the skull and skeleton of an old and arthritic Neanderthal (upper skull).**

climates of the Ice Age. Modelling of climate change in Europe and western Asia through the last glaciation from around 70,000 years ago (see pp. 170–1) allows archaeologists to investigate the impact of climate change on both the Neanderthals and the incoming Cro-Magnon modern humans. Both groups retreated in the face of glacial conditions, but as the climate improved the Neanderthals had to recover from a very much reduced population, while waves of Cro-Magnons with improved technology in the form of clothing and toolkits were able to recolonize former Neanderthal territories more rapidly.

Of stocky, muscular build, the Neanderthals had brains as big as ours but which may have been arranged and "hardwired" slightly differently. They probably had speech but no sophisticated language. We also know, from isotope geochemistry (see p. 164) and the animal debris that they left behind at their encampments, that they were mainly carnivorous. Operating in small groups or clans, they hunted big game, from mammoths to horses and wild cattle, and a variety of smaller animals. They may also have gathered bird eggs and berries in season.

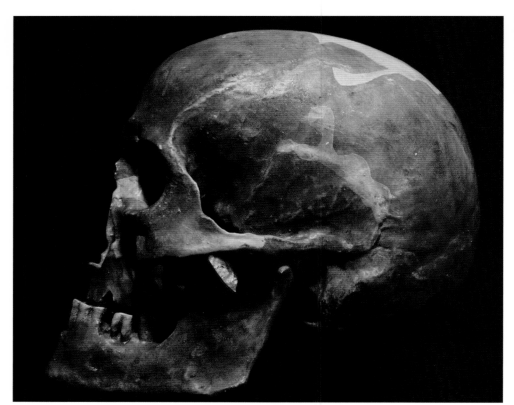

For many years experts debated whether modern Europeans were descended from Neanderthals. The possibility that they might have been emerged when it was proved that the two groups had lived in the same geographical areas for more than 10,000 years. The question has now been finally resolved by the use of DNA analysis, which has proved that Neanderthals have distinctive genetic markers and are thus a separate species. As these markers are not present in the DNA of modern Europeans, it suggests that interbreeding, if it happened at all, was neither widespread nor successful.

Reimagining the Neanderthals

The word "Neanderthal" is sometimes used today as a term of abuse for anyone who has stupid or uncouth tendencies. But the idea that Neanderthals were thugs arose largely from a mistaken interpretation of an ancient skeleton found in France in 1908. The bones belonged to a Neanderthal of about 45 years old: by the standards of the age, this was an elderly man, and his body was crippled and distorted by arthritis. His disabilities were reflected in the reconstruction carried out by French anatomist Marcellin Boule: the image he created of a thick-necked, round-shouldered, stooping creature with an ape-like divergent big toe has been perpetuated ever since.

Yet recent re-analysis of the Neanderthal skeleton shows that the curvature of the thick-walled limbs was a response to a powerful musculature associated with a very energetic lifestyle. Skeletal damage is concentrated in the upper torso and limbs, probably as a result of hunting medium to large game while armed only with stout hand-held spears.

There is also evidence that towards the end of their existence the Neanderthals were in the process of making cultural developments in their techniques of manufacturing tools and personal ornaments, and that they were occasionally burying their dead – these practices are all performed by modern humans and are part of the definition of human culture. Some experts suggested that in doing these things the Neanderthals were merely mimicking humans, but there is now evidence of these developments in areas where the Neanderthals had no contact with our ancestors.

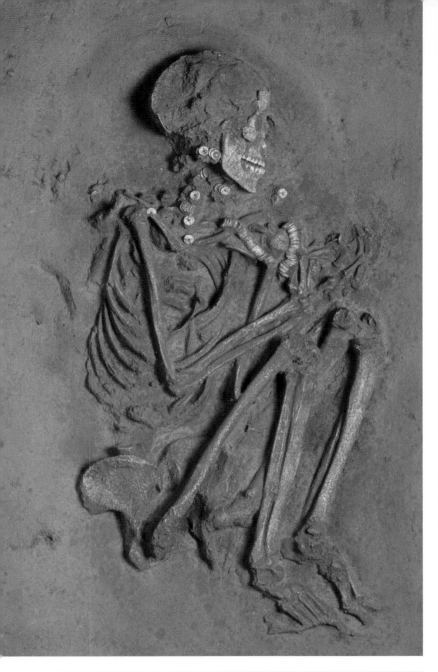

Cro-Magnon man

In 1868 construction of a new railway cutting near the town of Les Eyzies in the Dordogne region of southern France exposed a number of bones and stone tools. The site lay beneath a cliff overhang which formed a natural rock shelter known locally as the Cro-Magnon.

French archaeologist Louis Lartet (1840–99) found that the bones included those of at least five modern-looking humans who had been buried with stone tools and ornaments made of perforated shells and animal teeth and the bones of Ice Age animals such as reindeer, lion, and mammoth.

A similar find had been made about 40 years before, in 1822 at Paviland Cave in South Wales, but palaeontologist William Buckland (1784–1856) missed the full significance of his discovery. Buckland, a clergyman who lectured on geology at Oxford University, firmly believed that investigation of the prehistoric past would verify the account of the Creation and the Flood as described in the Old Testament book of Genesis. He could only explain the Paviland burial as that of a local Welsh tribeswoman who lived in Roman times. We now know that the skeleton is that of a Cro-Magnon modern human who lived some 28,000 years ago.

Lartet was not so hampered by dogma. He realized that his Cro-Magnon find was unequivocal evidence of modern humans living in Europe alongside Ice Age animals much earlier than anyone had ever previously imagined.

MAMMOTH ARCHITECTURE
Mezhirich, Ukraine

On the frozen plains of Ice Age northern Europe, mammoth bones and tusks made handy building materials, as the unique huts at Mezhirich show.

Mezhirich is a famous Upper Palaeolithic open-air site where archaeologists discovered five huts made from mammoth bones; a painted mammoth skull was also found. It is located in Ukraine at the confluence of the Rosava and Ros' rivers, about 12 km (8 miles) upstream from where the latter joins the Dnepr River. The occupation layer is on a terrace and dates to between 19,280 and 11,700 years ago. More than 500 sq m (598 sq yd) were uncovered out of a total of perhaps 10,000 sq m (2½ acres). Among the ancient relics discovered there were the bones of a mammoth and a hare, together with a collection of stone tools.

Built to suit the climate

The construction of Dwelling No. 1 is typical of the site – 25 mammoth skulls were placed in a semicircle to form the interior base wall, their frontal bones facing inwards and their tusk sockets buried in the ground. These were supplemented by 20 mammoth pelvises and 10 limb bones, which were also fixed into the ground. On this foundation were 12 more skulls, 30 shoulder blades, 20 femurs, 15 pelvises, and segments of 7 vertebral columns. Higher still were 35 tusks, which were probably used to hold down the hides that formed the roof.

The outer wall of the hut was formed from 95 lower jaws, all placed chin-downwards one on top of the other in a herringbone pattern. No one is sure of the meaning or purpose of this design. It may have acted as a retaining wall or held down

the hides that covered the shelter; alternatively, it may have provided a layer of heat insulation between the hides and the snow that drifted against the jaw bones. Then again, it may simply have been a supply of raw material and fuel. Mammoth leg bones were placed upright at the small entrance to the hut. Inside was a mammoth skull decorated with zigzags and dots of red ochre, which one Soviet archaeologist interpreted as representing flames and sparks.

The other dwellings at Mezhirich are variations on this basic theme, with jaws placed chin-upwards or a range of different bone types in the base wall. Some of the bones have holes drilled in them. Pegs of bone or wood may have been inserted into them to hold the structure together, but it is also possible that the holes were used for hanging garments out to dry, for drying meat, or even as peepholes.

Constructing the huts

The quantity of materials required to make these structures varied. Dwelling No. 1 contains some 385 bones weighing a total of 21,000 kg (8¾ tons); other huts at the site contain 15,000–19,000 kg (6¼–8 tons) of bone. Archaeologists have estimated that it would have taken ten people at least five or six days to build dwelling No. 1, and four or five days for each of the others.

The labour involved in collecting the bones and assembling the huts was enormous. A skinned and dried mammoth skull with relatively small tusks weighs a minimum of 100 kg (220 lb) and

Key Facts: Mezhirich

Location: Ukraine	1966–74, and N. L. Korniets and M. I. Gladkih 1976–81
Date: Upper Palaeolithic, 19,280–11,700 years BC	**Display:** Palaeontological Museum, Kiev
Discovered: 1965	
Explored by: Soviet archaeologists I. G. Pidoplichko from	

often much more, while the other large bones of the animal are by no means light. But the dwellings were worth the effort because they were sturdy and durable.

Raw materials

It is obvious that a huge number of mammoth skeletons was available in the area. While some of the bones used in the dwellings might conceivably have come from kills or even from mass-drives by the occupants, it is more likely that most of the building materials came from mammoths that were already dead, either from natural causes or predation by other animals. Rivers and streams would also have created natural accumulations of bones which would have remained unburied and relatively fresh.

The Mezhirich site contains the remains of at least 149 mammoths. Some of the bones might have been accumulated gradually over the years, but the 25 skulls that form the foundation of Dwelling No. 1 must have been collected before construction began. If the greater part of the material came from natural mammoth "cemeteries" or accumulations of bones, then it must be assumed that these lay close to the site.

Among the objects recovered at the site were mattocks – chisel-like tools – made from sections of tusk and bevelled at one end to make a massive kind of spatula that may have been used to dig pits in the hard ground. Also discovered were narrow ivory chippings which had been sharpened into stabbing or thrusting weapons.

Right: **Excavations at Mezhirich in 1970 uncovered the remains of another mammoth-bone dwelling (foreground), with external hearths just beyond and a refuse pit at the far end of the trench.**

PEOPLING THE AMERICAS
Monte Verde, Chile

One of the greatest puzzles of archaeology has been when and how the first humans came to North and South America. A site in Chile provided a possible answer.

Archaeologists have long believed that the first settlers of the Americas came from Siberian Asia. During the most recent Ice Age's glacial maxima – periods when the climate was at its coldest – sea levels fell so far that the Bering Strait between Siberia and Alaska was dry land. This would certainly have allowed the migration of both animals and humans into the Americas. But when did these people arrive?

The earliest evidence

In the 1930s, distinctive stone tools and spearheads associated with the bones of extinct Ice Age bison were discovered at Clovis and Folsom, New Mexico. These finds indicated that North America had been settled by proficient big-game hunters at least 10,000 years ago. But had there been even earlier waves of migration and settlement? In the late 1970s, Tom Dillehay, an archaeologist at the University of Kentucky, followed up reports of strange animal bones that had been found at Monte Verde in Chile, South America. A 20-year excavation programme uncovered a streamside settlement with two rows of skin-covered wooden dwellings and a wealth of artefacts which have been dated to between 14,500 and 13,800 years old. By comparison, none of the artefacts associated with the Clovis people (see pp. 28–9) is more than 13,500 years old.

The periodic flooding of the adjacent stream had preserved the wooden foundations of the primitive dwellings in peat which had also protected many other organic artefacts from destruction through oxidation. The excavations revealed a wealth of information about the habits and lifestyle of the pioneer inhabitants of South America. Discoveries included work surfaces, hearths, cooking debris, wooden tools, pieces of hide, and knotted fibres. There were also flaked stone tools, but these were quite different in style from those of the Clovis and Folsom peoples. Among the animal bones uncovered at Monte Verde were the remains of the extinct elephant-like mastodon.

At first there was great scepticism about the age of the Monte Verde site, and questions were asked about how long it would have taken for its people to have got that far south. The journey from the Bering crossing point is some 15,000 km (9300 miles); even with a persistent annual southerly migration of 5 km (3 miles) a year it would have taken at least 3000 years to reach Chile. This implied that humans had entered North America at least 17,000 years ago, at which time most of northern North America was covered by a great ice sheet. It is now thought more likely that the Monte Verde people crossed from Siberia before the last glacial at least 22,000 years ago.

Other sites

Monte Verde is not the only pre-Clovis site of human occupation in the Americas. In recent years there have been several new finds, especially in Alaska and along the island-studded Pacific coast of Canada. The oldest is perhaps in the limestone caves of the Bluefish River in Yukon,

---

Key Facts: Monte Verde

Location: 800 km (500 miles) south of Santiago, southern Chile, South America

Age: 14,500 years

Discovered: Late 1970s by a local farmer

Explored by: Tom Dillehay, University of Kentucky

Display: Dallas Museum of Natural History, Texas, USA

Left: Wooden pegs associated with riverside dwellings around 14,000 years old at Monte Verde in southern Chile and preserved by oxygen-poor muds.

where Canadian archaeologist Jean Cinq-Mars found microliths – tiny stone flakes – and a variety of animal bones, some of which may have been modified by human hands. They are dated at around 15,750 years old. If that is right, there is still the question of how the people survived in this region given the glacial conditions at the time. One suggestion is that there may have been an ice-free coastal corridor from around 16,000 until 12,000 years ago, when rising sea level made it impassable. But by then another inland corridor may well have opened up. There may also have been an iceless "freeway" between the glaciers of the Rocky Mountains and the vast interior ice sheet. Along this route migratory animals and people from Siberia made their way south into the interior of North America and on down to South America. The discovery and colonization of the Americas may have happened largely by chance, as the Ice Age human hunters followed game from Siberia and eventually found themselves in a new continent.

Kennewick Man

On 31 July 1996 the well-preserved skeleton of a middle-aged man was washed out of bankside sediments along the Columbia River onto land belonging to the US Army Corps of Engineers at Kennewick in Washington State. The find caused huge controversy for two reasons.

First, the skull, dated at around 9300 years old, seems to display non-Paleoindian features: some people claim that it is Caucasoid; others, perhaps more plausibly, that it is Asian. Second, four Native American peoples regarded the man as their ancestor, and demanded that his bones be ceremonially reinterred. Archaeologists opposed the claim. Eventually the Ninth Circuit Court of Appeals in San Francisco found that it was impossible to establish a relationship between the natives and the remains. It ruled in the archaeologists' favour and denied the Native Americans leave to have the decision reviewed by the US Supreme Court.

The matter did not end there, however: scientists are now having to fight for the right to take samples of DNA from the Kennewick Man in order to ascertain his true relationships. The skeleton – which consists of 380 bones and bone fragments – is currently stored at the Burke Museum in Seattle.

Examination and analysis have shown that their owner suffered a stab wound in the hip while he was a teenager: he was struck with such force that the stone tip of the assault weapon broke off and became embedded in his pelvis. Nevertheless, he survived. New bone eventually grew over the stone point and he lived until he was between 45 and 55 – a normal lifespan for a person of that period and environment. Surprisingly, he does not appear to have suffered from arthritis, which would normally be expected in someone who had sustained such a serious injury.

THE CLOVIS HUNTERS
Clovis, USA

Finds at Clovis and other sites show that the first Americans were nomads who made sophisticated stone tools and hunted big game.

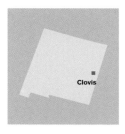

The earliest migrants to the Americas were Paleoindian hunters who occupied Monte Verde in Chile and are known as the pre-Clovis people. Their better known successors included the Clovis, Folsom, and Goshen hunters.

Little is known about the Clovis people, probably because they were relatively few in number and highly mobile hunters who operated in small groups. They left few traces – apart, that is, from the remarkable stone projectile points that they used in hunting and the bones of the animals that they killed for food and clothing.

The finds at Folsom

The first evidence of early human settlement in the Americas was discovered in 1908 by George McJunkin, who uncovered some large animal bones and curiously fashioned stones embedded in a dry creek near Folsom, New Mexico. McJunkin kept the finds at his ranch for some 17 years before they came to the attention of Jesse Figgins, director of the Natural History Museum in Denver, Colorado, who identified the bones as those of an extinct bison of the late Pleistocene Ice Age. Figgins then visited the original site and found two finely worked stone spear points.

By 1927 Figgins felt sufficiently confident of the association of the extinct animal remains and the spear points to show the site to other American experts. One of them, Barnum Brown of the American Museum of Natural History, declared that the Folsom find provided "the answer to the antiquity of man in the New World".

But Brown's claim was over ambitious. A few years later a couple of amateur collectors found more stone points and bison bones at Clovis, another site in New Mexico. Shortly afterwards further points and bones were found in association at Blackwater Draw, Arizona, then at Dent, Colorado, where the bones were those of a mammoth. In the mid 1950s archaeologists showed that the Folsom and Clovis points had been made by different methods. More recently the Folsom culture has been dated at between 13,000 and 15,000 years ago. Although this is earlier than had previously been thought, it is still more recent than the Clovis culture, which is now known to have been up to 13,000 years ago.

Further Clovis sites were discovered in the 1950s. These included one at Naco in southern Arizona that featured a mammoth skeleton in close association with eight Clovis points. The bones showed evidence of regrowth after having been pierced: the animal had evidently survived for some time after the attack. The remains of eight mammoths and a dozen spear points were then discovered at the nearby Lehner Ranch: this find showed that the whole area had been a favoured hunting site for the Clovis people.

Big game hunters

The Clovis people were almost certainly nomads who wandered until they found a rich source of game, killed what they needed, and moved on when their quarry became scarce. Their only competition came from other predatory species,

Key Facts: Clovis

Location: Eastern New Mexico, USA

Age: Around 13,000–12,000 years ago

Discovered: 1929 by amateur collectors

Explored by: Father Conrad Bilgery of Regis College, Denver

Display: Colorado Museum of Natural History

Above: **James J Hester** from the Museum of New Mexico demonstrates the famous sequence of sedimentary layers at Blackwater Locality No. 1 Site, near Clovis in New Mexico. Some 13,000 years ago a springfed waterhole attracted animals such as bison and mammoth and their predators, the Paleoindian Clovis people.

Left: Paleoindian stone tools from the Blackwater Locality No. 1 Site include characteristic Clovis-style points and blades, Folsom age points, and Portales age parallel-flaked points.

such as big cats and packs of wolves. The humans had no desire or need to settle in a single location and become sedentary. As a result, there is little information about the details of their lives.

Fine craftsmanship

We only have partial remains of their weapons, and archaeologists have had difficulty in reconstructing them. The distinctive Clovis points were skilfully carved out of flint, obsidian, and quartzite – hard minerals with a glass-like consistency and sharp edges. As these natural materials are uncommon, and indeed completely absent from some areas, the Clovis people must have had some trouble in finding them. Caches of Clovis points have been found that were either abandoned stores or ritual religious offerings of the hunters' most precious possessions.

Each point was mounted on a short wooden foreshaft which could then be attached to a hand-held thrusting spear, a lighter throwing spear, or an atlatl, a kind of throwing stick. Experiments show that the atlatl effectively extends the length of the throwing arm, giving even light spears great penetrative power. Spears of this type were typically slightly more than 2 m (7 ft) in length, weighed about 475 g (16 oz), and could be thrown about 20 m (22 yd). They enabled the hunter to keep a safe distance from the quarry and deliver a telling blow – the stone-pointed spear could penetrate even the tough hide of a mammoth and slide between its ribs to pierce the lungs or other vital organs. Yet archaeological evidence shows that several hits were usually required to kill a mammoth, and that some survived such attacks. The prey was rarely killed outright, but ran off wounded. The hunters would then follow the trail of blood to the creature's final refuge.

Paleoindian hunters are sometimes thought to have contributed to the extinction of the big game animals of the North American Ice Age – mammoth, bison, and horse. It is true that Clovis

kill sites such as those at Blackwater Draw and Dent contain what appear to be whole families of mammoths – far more than the people would have needed to eat. Yet recent isotope studies on the bones have revealed that the animals were slaughtered over several hunting seasons. The early humans may have been guilty of overkill, but they were almost certainly not entirely responsible for the demise of these species – the main reason was probably changing climate.

Above: Archaeologists trying to save artefacts, bone, and information about the Clovis and Folsom cultures before it was bulldozed away in 1963 so that the underlying gravel could be sold for road construction.

ÖTZI, THE ICE MAN
Otzal Alps, Italy

The 1991 discovery in a glacier of a well-preserved Neolithic corpse was one of the most spectacular archaeological finds of recent years.

EUROPE Austria

Otzaler Alpen

Nicknamed "Ötzi, the Ice Man", the 5200-year-old frozen cadaver now preserved in Bolzano, Italy, and the objects found with it, have given remarkable insights into the life of a Neolithic hunter. But the find has also led to some wild speculation about the manner of his death.

Out of the deep-freeze

On 19 September 1991, two German hikers, Helmut and Erika Simon, were passing the end of the Similaun glacier at around 3200 m (10,500ft) above sea level as they crossed the Ötzal Alps between Austria and Italy. There they came across a human body embedded face down in the ice.

They assumed it was the corpse of a climber who had died some years previously. Despite his wife's protestations that it would be disrespectful, Helmut took a photograph. They reported their discovery to the caretaker of the next lodge they passed, and he alerted the local police. Only three weeks earlier the bodies of a couple who were lost climbing in 1934 had been discovered in the region, so the police assumed that this was a similar case.

When the body – that of a male – was first examined, it seemed emaciated and strangely dressed, but the skin was relatively "fresh" and the eyeballs and pupils could still be seen. Without too much care or ceremony the police dug it out of the ice, initially using a stick which they found nearby. The implement was brittle and soon broke, which was doubly unfortunate because it turned out to be the dead man's bow.

The original clothing was torn from the corpse as it was extracted from the ice, but all the material was recovered along with a variety of other items found lying around. Then, when the body was forced into a coffin, its left arm was broken. Luckily, however, the corpse remained frozen as it was transported by car and plane to the morgue at the University of Innsbruck, Austria. There it was examined by Dr Konrad Spindler of the university's Research Institute for Alpine Studies.

The copper blade on the man's axe resembled similar weapons dating from the Bronze Age. Spindler immediately suspected that the body was at least 4000 years old, but radiocarbon dating later proved that it was 1200 years older. This was clearly an exceptional find. Spindler remarked that when he first saw the body he "felt like [Howard] Carter when he found Tutankhamen". He immediately set about assembling an international research team to examine the body.

A question of ownership

Meanwhile the prehistoric body in the ice – by this time nicknamed Ötzi – had become front-page news around the world. And in no time at all the find was beset with problems. For one thing, it was unclear whether the corpse had been recovered from Austria or Italy, so the two countries went to law to establish ownership.

A careful resurvey of the find site revealed that Ötzi's body lay just 100 m (110 yd) on

Key Facts: Ötzi

Location: Italian-Austrian border in the Ötzal Alps

Age: 5200 years

Discovered: 1991 by Helmut and Erika Simon

Examined by: Dr Konrad Spindler and team of scientists

Display: South Tyrol Museum of Archaeology, Bolzano

the Italian side of the border with Austria. Consequently, in April 2003 the body was transported from Innsbruck to the South Tyrol Museum of Archaeology in Bolzano, Italy, where it was placed in a specially constructed cold-store. The corpse is kept at a constant temperature of 6°C (43°F) and a humidity of over 99 per cent

There was also the question of compensation for the Simons. Helmut Simon spent much time and effort trying to assert his rights as Ötzi's discoverer. He originally claimed US$300,000, which he believed represented 25 per cent of the body's value. Although he was officially recognized in 2003 as the original finder, his claim for compensation was put off until November 2004. Before the case came to court, however, Simon was killed in a climbing accident on Austria's Gaiskarkogel peak on 23 October 2004.

The man and his possessions

Ötzi was between 25 and 35 years old when he died, and stood 1.6 m (5 ft 3in) tall and probably weighed about 50 kg (110 lb), although with the

dehydration of the natural freeze-dry conditions in the ice he now weighs less than 20 kg (44 lb). Originally he had dark hair and a beard, but the hair has since fallen out.

Apparently there was hair lying around on the ice where he was found, but nobody thought to collect it until it was too late. His body tattoos are of great interest: short parallel sets of four blue lines and small crosses on his back, knees, ankles, and hands. They may have indicated his tribal allegiance or his social status.

When finally gathered together and examined, the Ice Man's belongings turned out to be numerous, and gave a vivid glimpse into the distant past. They included a copper axehead with a wooden shaft, a bow and quiver with arrows, a bent hazelwood frame, a "backpack" or pannier made of two larch boards and cords, two birch-bark containers, a stone knife with a woven sheath, a longish leather pouch containing a flint scraper and a piece of resin which might have been used as firelighter, a bag containing fungus, possibly for medicinal use, a tassle or necklace

Above: **This emaciated corpse found in a Tyrolean alpine glacier in 1991 was so well preserved that it was initially mistaken for that of a modern human, but the subsequent recovery of a bow, arrows, and a bronze-headed axe suggested a much greater age. Radiocarbon dating confirms that the Ice Man is 5200 years old.**

with a stone bead, and a piece of bone set in a
thick wooden peg which was used for retouching
flint arrowheads.

His 1.8-m (5 ft 11-in) longbow made of yew
was unfinished and of a basic but efficient design
that was continuously used until medieval times.
The deerskin quiver contained 14 arrows, each
85 cm (33 in) long and made of dogwood and
guelder-rose. Two of the arrows had feather
flights and were tipped with flint points.

The axe is the most sophisticated item and has
a 9-cm (4-in) blade of copper bound with animal
sinews and birch sap glue to an 80-cm (30-in)
yew handle. The axehead was cast from molten
copper poured into a prepared mould, then
further shaped with a hammer. By comparison,
the knife is very primitive in design with a flint
blade, ash handle, and grass sheath.

Ötzi's clothing was well designed for his
lifestyle, being made largely of skin and fur, plus
a grass cape for further warmth on the mountain.
(He also had fleas, which were probably a
common parasite.) His shoes had bearskin soles,
deerskin insteps, and a combination of calf and
lindenbark uppers, stuffed with grass for further
insulation and laced up with leather and grass.

Examination of the contents of his gut shows
that his last meals consisted firstly of some ibex
meat and cereal grains, followed by red deer and
more grain. From the presence of the eggs of
parasitical whipworms, he probably suffered a
fairly severe intestinal disorder which could have
given him diarrhoea or even dysentery. The birch
fungi he was carrying may have been collected
and eaten in an attempt to combat his stomach
problems. Pine pollen in his gut suggests that the
time of his death was late spring or early summer
and that he had recently passed through
coniferous forest and drunk stream water.

How did he die?

The find attracted a great deal of ill-informed
speculation, especially about the circumstances of
his death. Initially, reconstruction of Ötzi's last
hours saw him minding his own business and
crossing a remote pass high in the mountains

when he was overtaken by a sudden storm. He took shelter in a rock hollow, but despite being a tough and fit 30-year-old with protective clothing he froze to death. His core body temperature dropped quickly and so his body tissues were soon freeze-dried. Snow drifted over the corpse in sufficient depth that it was not subsequently exposed to any scavenging animals but became buried deeper by successive winter snowfalls that turned to ice around him.

But this simple interpretation has to be reconsidered. Some early x-rays appeared to show that he had broken ribs on his right side. This gave rise to the theory that he had died from injuries sustained in a fight or a fall. Then in June 2001 x-rays of the body revealed the point of a stone arrowhead embedded in his left shoulder, but the images did not confirm that his ribs had been broken. A year later there was a further discovery of a cut in the palm of his right hand which penetrated to the bone. While there is clearly no doubt that he had been shot in the shoulder by an arrow at some time and damaged

his hand, the order of events is not clear. But that has not stopped all manner of stories being concocted to explain the wounds. He may indeed have been involved in some conflict in which he was injured, and he may have been fleeing the scene when he was overtaken by a storm or simply bled to death.

Where did he come from?

Recent scientific analysis and comparison of the detailed isotope chemistry of Ötzi's teeth, bones, and intestines with that of soil and water from a wide area of the Tyrolean Alps has provided clues to his origins. The closest "fit" suggests that he came from the Eisack Valley area around the present-day Italian village of Feldthurns but spent most of his life in the Lower Vinschgau valleys slightly further north and probably never moved much more than 60 km (37 miles) from his birthplace. DNA analysis shows that his ancestry lay with late Palaeolithic hunters, rather than the incoming Neolithic farmers who later colonized Europe.

Above: **An essential part of Ötzi's clothing was this bear skin cap, which would have been tied below his chin to keep it in place. A great deal of body heat is lost from the top of the head and such an insulating cap would have been an effective means of conserving much of that heat.**

2

TOMBS & BURIAL SITES

All societies need to dispose of their dead. But in the ancient world this practical need was also a religious requirement. The dead were thought to need a rite of passage, usually a cremation or a burial, then somewhere suitable to rest in anticipation of the next life. Many societies felt that the provision of an elaborate, expensive grave was a valid investment and a good means of emphasizing the earthly status that they fully expected would be maintained beyond death. Their elite tombs, and their more humble graves, today provide archaeologists with fascinating insights into the rituals and beliefs of the long-vanished past.

The earliest peoples were nomadic hunter-gatherers who have left us no permanent dwelling sites, and no burial grounds. Occasional, isolated finds of their skeletons buried with artefacts pose a problem for the archaeologist. Are these the first signs of funeral ritual and the provision of goods for the afterlife, or are they simply evidence that the grave diggers dropped one of their tools as they worked? Could some of these "graves" even be accidental burials – the result of an unfortunate rockfall at the back of a cave, perhaps?

With the onset of a settled way of life came the need to formalize arrangements for the disposal of the dead. Cemetery sites soon followed, their architecture determined by the developing religious beliefs. These cemeteries were usually, but not always, situated away from the houses and fields of the living.

Numerous ancient societies interred their dead with grave goods – gold, jewellery, clothing, precious objects, and more humdrum artefacts – either because they believed that the deceased would have a use for such things in the afterlife or because they felt it appropriate to remove the dead person's possessions from society. Unfortunately, tombs and graves packed with valuables make easy targets for thieves, and grave robbery, often described as "the world's second-oldest profession", has been a problem ever since people were first buried with valuables. The most notorious examples of such desecration occurred in Egypt. Tutankhamen is the only pharaoh whose body remained undisturbed in its sarcophagus in the Valley of the Kings. His tomb was robbed twice in antiquity, but when it was opened in the 20th century it still yielded a vast, unimagined array of riches. He was a short-lived and minor ruler: we can only imagine what might have been included alongside the bodies of Egypt's greatest pharaohs, Amenhotep III and Ramesses II.

The first archaeologists were in some cases themselves little better than grave robbers. They deliberately focused on tombs and cemeteries which were relatively easy to excavate, and which offered the promise of rich pickings. All too often they studied tomb art and architecture and collected jewellery and precious metals, while discarding the seemingly insignificant tomb contents, bodies included, which did not interest them.

These early excavators assumed that they had every right to open tombs, seize grave goods, and interfere with the deceased. The long-dead were classed as curiosities; they were objects for display, rather than fellow human beings, while their property was taken on a "finders keepers" basis. The late 20th century saw a change in approach. It is now rare for archaeologists deliberately to seek out burial sites. Cemeteries are today considered in a wider cultural context, while the dead, when they have to be disturbed, are treated with appropriate respect.

Tombs and burial sites can be extremely informative. At a practical level they can tell us about the architectural and artistic skills of their builders, while the goods they contain can supply information about crafts, technologies, and access to resources. At a more general level they can act as a guide to the religious beliefs of their occupants. Human remains can provide a wealth of information; modern scientific techniques such as x-ray analysis, CAT scans, and DNA testing have given us an unprecedented understanding of the health, genealogies, and ethnicities of the peoples of the past.

But we have to be careful. We cannot assume that objects deliberately included in a tomb are objects that were routinely used in daily life – they may well be atypical goods, specifically designed for the afterlife. Nor can we assume that those individuals buried in expensive tombs are typical of the population as a whole. We must expect that the owners of the grandest tombs belonged to the elite of society. As such, we must expect them to have been better fed and, having been less vulnerable to workplace accidents and diseases caused by overcrowded living conditions, to have had a greater life expectancy than their less fortunate contemporaries.

STAIRWAYS TO HEAVEN
Giza, Egypt

A huge workforce laboured to build the Giza pyramids, impressive tombs for three pharaohs and embodiments of ancient Egyptian beliefs in the afterlife.

The pharaohs of Old Kingdom Egypt (c. 2575–2134 BC believed that carrying out the correct religious rituals would allow their spirits to be reborn after death. Then they would either become undying stars in the night sky or sail as eternal passengers in the shining boat that the sun god Re piloted across the heavens each day. Their subjects, whose spirits were not strong enough to leave the earth, were condemned to spend eternity sealed in their cramped and sandy graves. Naturally, those who could afford it invested in large, stone-lined tombs that would allow them a comfortable afterlife, with plenty of storage space for the goods they would need. Meanwhile, when poorer members of society died they were wrapped in matting, and buried in simple pit graves marked by raised mounds of sand representing the mound of creation.

Building a celestial stairway

The pyramid shape had special significance for the pharaohs. It was a formalized version of the mound of creation, and provided a stairway, or ramp, up which the dead king would reach the heavens. Architecturally, it was a good choice of shape for a people unaccustomed to building in stone; it was just as imposing, and far less liable to collapse, than a tall tower, while its sides, covered with the finest white limestone, reflected the rays of the sun like a polished mirror.

But the pyramid was only one part of the king's mortuary complex. Each pyramid site also had a burial chamber within or beneath the pyramid masonry; a mortuary temple where the cult of the dead king could be celebrated; a causeway linking the desert pyramid to the canal; and a valley temple opening on to a small harbour. The complex of the Great Pyramid built by King Khufu (known to the Greeks as Cheops) also included a tiny subsidiary pyramid, three small queens' pyramids, and a series of boat burials. Khufu's pyramid is today the only surviving Wonder of the Ancient World.

Khufu was not the first king to build a pyramid; that honour goes to the 3rd-dynasty King Djoser, who built his Step Pyramid at the already ancient cemetery site of Sakkara in northern Egypt. But Khufu was the first king to raise a pyramid on the Giza Plateau. He was later joined there by his son Khaefre (Chephren) and his grandson Menkaure (Mycerinus). Lack of space forced subsequent pharaohs to build their pyramids elsewhere.

The pyramid workforce

The Great Pyramid contains more than two million blocks of limestone. To build it, Khufu recruited a permanent workforce of about 5000 specialists – master architects, masons, engineers, builders, and scribes – together with a temporary workforce of up to 20,000 conscripts who lived and worked for several months on site before returning home. Essentials such as food, clothing, and healthcare were provided by the state, and those who died at Giza were buried outside the workmen's village.

Key Facts: The Giza pyramids

Location: The Giza Plateau, Cairo, Egypt

Date: 4th dynasty, c. 2575–2465 BC

Discovered: The pyramids' internal architecture was largely rediscovered during the 19th century

Explored by: A series of archaeologists from the medieval period to the present day, including Giovanni Battista Caviglia and Flinders Petrie

Display: Open to the public, but access to certain areas may be restricted

As the dynastic age ended, the Giza pyramid complexes slowly deteriorated. The temples and causeways were stripped of their valuable stone, which was reused in the construction of medieval Cairo. The pyramids themselves remained substantially intact, although they lost their outer casings to the same stone robbers. Soon the original purpose of the pyramids was forgotten, and most of the very few early Western travellers who made their way to Egypt believed them to be the granaries built by the Old Testament Joseph to guard against the years of famine. Those who knew that they were tombs were frustratingly unable to locate their entrances.

Early explorers

In the 8th century AD Caliph el-Mamun determined to find a way into the Great Pyramid that was, he mistakenly believed, filled with treasure. Having tried and failed to crack the stone blocks with boiling-hot vinegar, he used a battering ram to force his way in. He made his way along an ascending corridor until he reached the burial chamber. Here, it was rumoured, he discovered Khufu's gold-clad mummy lying in his coffin, a sword in his hand and a ruby on his forehead. However, given that the Great Pyramid is known to have been opened and emptied over a thousand years earlier, this seems very unlikely.

The Caliph left the pyramid open and accessible to all. Subsequent explorations conducted by John Greaves (1646), Nathaniel Davison (1763), and Captain Giovanni Battista Caviglia (1816–36) confirmed that the pyramid contained three chambers (the burial chamber, also known as the "King's Chamber"; the "Queen's Chamber"; and the "Subterranean Chamber") linked together by a system of passageways. This disappointed many archaeologists. Surely there must be more chambers hidden within the masonry? Explorers continued to search for them, and it was not until 1837, when Colonel Richard

Above: **The three pyramids belonging to the queens of King Menkaure are dwarfed by those of kings Menkaure, Khaefre, and Khufu.**

Kofun, Japan

Above: The *haniwa* clay figures displayed on the outside of the Kofun tomb mounds took many forms. Here we have a soldier and a horse provided to guard and serve the deceased for all time.

The Kofun, or "Old Mound", protohistoric period in Japan lasted from *c.* AD 300–700 with archaeologists recognizing three main cultural phases: early (4th century), middle (5th century), and late (5th–7th centuries). This was the time that the country took its first steps towards political unity.

Throughout the Kofun period the ruling elite were interred in large stone burial chambers incorporated in earthen mounds or modified natural hills. Some of these tombs were surrounded by moats. Kofun tombs were built in many sizes and shapes, with either horizontal or vertical entrances. The most distinctive are the large, keyhole-shaped tombs built by the imperial family. The burial mound of the Emperor Nintoku covered an impressive 32 hectares (80 acres).

Inside the tombs the dead lay in large wooden coffins. Their grave goods included tools, weapons, mirrors, pottery, and personal goods. Outside the burial chamber, following the contours of the tomb mound and entrance, were numerous haniwa (literally: clay rings); unglazed clay figurines which took various forms, including simple clay cylinders, building, weapons, shields, men, women, and animals. Positioned so that they faced outwards, the *haniwa* were probably intended to protect and serve the deceased. Experts have suggested that they may have come to symbolize the unified Japan.

By the late Kofun period burial rites had been democratized and commoners, too, were being buried in Kofun tombs. But the introduction of Buddhism brought changes in funerary beliefs, causing the elite to abandon their Kofun tombs by 538 AD. Kofun tombs survived in more remote regions until the late 7th century.

Howard Vyse conducted the first thorough examination of the internal structure of the Great Pyramid, that the truth was more or less accepted.

In 1880, the young English archaeologist Flinders Petrie carried out the first scientific survey of the Great Pyramid. After two seasons of survey and structural examination using home-made equipment, he was able to prove that Khufu's builders were capable of working with extreme precision. The Great Pyramid stands 146.59 m (480 ft) high, with a slope of 51°50'40". Its sides, varying by less than 5 cm (2 in), are orientated almost exactly towards true north. Petrie's survey was so accurate that it is still used by archaeologists today.

The second and third Giza pyramids

Khaefre's pyramid has a simplified internal architecture, with no chambers within the pyramid masonry. Instead, the subterranean burial chamber was cut into the bedrock before a solid pyramid was erected on top. The pyramid entrance was so well hidden that many experts thought that there was no way in. Then, in 1818, Giovanni Battista Belzoni found a concealed doorway not, as had been expected, in the dead centre of the north face, but slightly to the east of centre. Belzoni made his way to the burial chamber, where he found the king's granite sarcophagus already open, and its sliding lid broken in two. The pyramid had been robbed in antiquity, resealed, then robbed again by Arabs who, having failed to find the original entrance, made their own tunnel.

Menkaure's pyramid was explored by Colonel Vyse who, in his 1837 search for the entrance, used gunpowder to blast a tunnel through the masonry. The true entrance, part way up the north face, was discovered only later. Inside the burial chamber Vyse found a beautiful dark basalt sarcophagus. This was earmarked for the British Museum but was lost at sea in 1838 when the ship carrying it to Britain sank off the Spanish coast.

Above: The pharoah Menkaure, builder of the third Giza pyramid, stands between the goddess Hathor and a goddess representing one of the Egyptian provinces.

CITY OF THE ATEN
Amarna, Egypt

The pharaoh Akhenaten promoted revolutionary religious ideas and built a new capital, Amarna, filled with splendid buildings decorated with beautiful artworks.

For thousands of years the kings of Egypt had worshipped a variety of deities, including Re the sun god, Osiris the god of the dead, and Amen the warrior god of Thebes. But in about 1353 BC the 18th dynasty pharaoh Akhenaten (formerly Amenhotep IV) broke with tradition. Abandoning the old pantheon, he dedicated himself to just one divine being. Egypt's new supreme deity, the Aten, was an asexual creator god, depicted as a faceless disc representing the divine light of the sun. Long, thin rays, tipped with small hands, allowed the Aten to hold out *ankh*, the symbol of life, to the royal family. This brief monotheistic episode is known as the Amarna period.

A new city for a new god

When Akhenaten came to the throne the court was based at Thebes. But Thebes was sacred to the god Amen. Akhenaten felt that the Aten needed his own city, a city untainted by the worship of the old gods. He therefore founded a new city on the east bank of the Nile in Middle Egypt, almost equidistant between Thebes and the ancient northern capital Memphis. Here at Amarna the royal court would live, die, and be buried.

Amarna, isolated and inconvenient, did not last long as a city: it was abandoned during the reign of Tutankhamen, after less than 30 years' occupation. Although much of its stone was later taken and reused by local builders, and many of its buildings have been lost under modern cultivation, Amarna today provides Egyptologists with their best-preserved dynastic city site.

Palaces, temples, and villas

Amarna was built to Akhenaten's divinely inspired plan. A long, straight Royal Road cut through the city from north to south, running parallel to the River Nile, which flowed on its western side. To the east a protective semicircle of cliffs provided an ideal location for the tombs. The city centre included a vast complex of administrative buildings known today as the Great Palace. The King's House was opposite the Great Palace and linked to it by a bridge. It was in the ruins of this administrative district that in 1887 a peasant woman stumbled across clay tablets bearing curious, wedge-shaped marks. Experts at first classed the tablets as forgeries, and it was not until the collection was almost entirely dispersed that it was realized that they were copies, in cuneiform script, of letters sent to and from the court.

The two Aten temples lay on the east side of the Royal Road, on opposite sides of the King's House. The Small Temple of Aten was a temple used for celebrations of the royal cult. The Great Temple of Aten was a confusing complex of buildings, shrines, and open spaces surrounded by an impressive enclosure wall. Much of this temple has been lost beneath a modern cemetery.

Akhenaten's courtiers had been compelled to abandon their Theban homes and relocate to Amarna, where they built luxurious villas in the suburbs. Here, too, were the homes and workshops of craftsmen, including the master sculptor Tuthmosis. It was in the ruins of his studio that, in 1912, a German expedition led by

Key Facts: Tell el-Amarna

Location: Amarna, Middle Egypt

Date: 18th dynasty, founded *c.* 1356 BC

Discovered: The city, workmen's village, and elite tombs were never lost. The royal tomb was officially discovered in 1892

Explored by: Numerous archaeologists including Flinders Petrie, Ludwig Borchardt, and John Pendlebury

Display: Open to the public, but access to certain areas and tombs may be restricted

Ludwig Borchardt discovered the world-famous bust of Queen Nefertiti, wife of Akhenaten, which is today housed in Berlin's Egyptian Museum.

The workmen's village

The Amarna workmen lived in a walled village in a little valley among the cliffs to the east of the main city. Each labourer was allocated a housing unit measuring 5 x 10 m (16 x 33 ft). There were 73 such houses built in six terraced rows facing onto five narrow streets. Outside the village wall some families built small private chapels where they could pay homage to their ancestors.

Akhenaten cut tombs for his nobility in the Amarna cliffs, where they formed two distinct groups on either side of the dry valley, or wadi, housing the large tomb and subsidiary graves that were to serve the royal family. Forty-five private tombs were started, but only 24 were inscribed, and only a few were in any way complete when the city was abandoned.

None of these private tombs yielded a mummy, and archaeologists agree that few, if any, were ever occupied. Any that were used – the tomb built for the elderly courtier Huya, perhaps – would have been emptied when the court returned to Thebes. To leave an unguarded burial in the Amarna cliffs would have been an open invitation to tomb robbers. The emptying of the tombs left them open to all; they were later used as houses, post-dynastic burial sites, and Coptic churches.

Exploring the tombs

In the absence of burials, archaeological interest has focused on the unique scenes that decorate the Amarna tombs. In 1902 Norman de Garis Davies cleaned the tombs of many centuries of accumulated rubbish and bat droppings, and began a detailed three-year study of their walls.

Under normal circumstances Egypt's New Kingdom nobles believed that they would leave the tomb to spend eternity in an afterlife ruled by Osiris. They therefore decorated their tombs with

Above: **The columned hall in the rock-cut tomb of the courtier Ay, the probable father of Queen Nefertiti, in the elite Amarna cemetery. Ay would later rule Egypt as Tutankhamen's successor.**

Right: The beautiful bust of Queen Nefertiti, recovered from the Amarna workshop of the sculptor Tuthmosis, is one of the highlights of Berlin's Egyptian Museum.

Above: **This carved stela shows the pharoah Akhenaten holding his eldest daughter Meritaten, while on the right Queen Nefertiti holds princesses Meketaten and Ankhesenpaaten.**

scenes of the gods, and of an afterlife that looks, to modern eyes, remarkably like ancient Egypt. But at Amarna no one believed in Osiris or his afterlife. In a throwback to the beliefs of the Old Kingdom, only the king and his immediate family would be able to leave the confines of tomb. The Amarna nobles were condemned to spend eternity as ghosts, haunting the Aten temples by day and shut in their tombs overnight.

The old religious images were inappropriate at Amarna. And so the nobles decorated their tombs with images of the royal family going about its daily duties. The most elaborately decorated tomb was built for the courtier Ay, father of Queen Nefertiti. Naturally, Nefertiti features prominently, and we see her standing beside Akhenaten on the palace balcony as he rewards his loyal supporters with golden necklaces. The tomb of Parennefer, "he who washes the hands of His Majesty", includes a balcony scene. In it the Aten, shining in the sky above the royal couple, touches Nefertiti in an almost sexual way; one long, thin ray is wound

round her waist, a small hand rests on her left breast, and a third hand appears round the side of her crown.

The royal tomb

There must have been many more than 45 families serving Akhenaten at Amarna, but although archaeologists have long known about the small graveyard associated with the workmen's village, the main cemetery has only recently been found to the north of the city; the site is still being investigated.

The royal tomb – the burial place of Akhenaten, Nefertiti, the secondary queen Kiya, and at least one of the royal princesses – was discovered by local people some time during the early 1880s, but remained a closely guarded secret until it had been thoroughly looted. An official "discovery" in 1892 revealed an unfinished, empty tomb with debris from the ransacked burials littering the floor. But it is possible that this tomb, too, might have been formally emptied by Tutankhamen when the court transferred to Thebes.

TUTANKHAMEN'S TOMB
Valley of the Kings, Egypt

The only Egyptian royal tomb to have survived intact into modern times is that of Tutankhamen. Its fabulous contents tell us much about Egypt's wealth and arts.

King Tutankhamen (1333–23 BC) ruled Egypt for a mere ten years during the late 18th dynasty, following immediately after the death of the heretic pharaoh Akhenaten. His brief reign was unexceptional and he had been more or less forgotten when the 1922 discovery of his almost intact tomb catapulted him into the ranks of Egypt's most famous kings.

The boy king

Tutankhamen never specifically names his parents; however, as he succeeded to the throne as an eight-year-old boy, it seems clear that he must already have been an important member of the royal family. He was most probably the son of Akhenaten by his secondary queen, Kiya.

Tutankhamen was raised at Amarna, the highly unorthodox court dedicated to the worship of one sole god, the Aten. But he, or more likely his advisers, was astute enough to realize that the new monotheistic religion had not been a success. Soon after his accession, the old gods were reinstated, the Aten was demoted, and the court left Middle Egypt and returned to the traditional southern capital, Thebes.

Almost immediately, the young king started to make plans for his own death. The pyramid form had been abandoned many centuries previously. Tutankhamen was to be buried in a discreet rock-cut tomb in the Valley of the Kings, the remote, dry valley on the west bank of the Nile opposite the great Karnak Temple of Amen where the kings of the 18th dynasty were buried.

Sudden death

The young king seemed set for a long and prosperous reign when suddenly, at only 18 years of age, he died. There has been much speculation about the cause of this early death, with some archaeologists suggesting that Tutankhamen might have been murdered, perhaps by a blow to the back of the head. But there is little direct evidence to substantiate this theory, and it is difficult to understand why any rival claimant to the throne would have waited ten years before eliminating Tutankhamen. Egyptians regarded regicide as a heinous offence against the gods, and it seems far more likely that Tutankhamen met an accidental death, perhaps as the result of a chariot crash.

Tutankhamen and his wife Ankhesenamen had had two stillborn daughters, but no surviving child. He was therefore succeeded by the elderly courtier Ay, father of the late Queen Nefertiti and grandfather of Queen Ankhesenamen. Tradition demanded that the new pharaoh should take responsibility for burying his predecessor. But work on Tutankhamen's elaborate tomb had only just got under way, and the structure simply could not be made ready in time. Ay was forced to bury Tutankhamen in what was probably his own tomb (known as KV 62), a simple two-chambered rock-cut tomb in the Valley of the Kings. The walls were hastily plastered and painted with images of Ay and the dead king, and Tutankhamen was laid to rest surrounded

Key Facts: Tomb KV 62

Location: Valley of the Kings, Egypt

Date: 18th dynasty, c. 1323 BC

Discovered: 4 November 1922

Explored by: Howard Carter

Display: The tomb is currently closed to the public. Many of the artefacts from the tomb are displayed in Cairo Museum.

by a rather random collection of grave goods, some of which had been originally intended for other members of the royal family.

The lost tomb

The doorway to Tutankhamen's tomb was blocked with stones, plastered over, and stamped with the cemetery seal. Twice in antiquity the tomb was robbed, restored by the high priests who looked after the royal cemetery, and resealed. Eventually, the tomb was entirely forgotten. When, almost two centuries after Tutankhamen's death, the pharaoh Ramesses VI built his own tomb slightly higher up the Valley slope, the debris from his excavations piled up in front of Tutankhamen's doorway, and his workmen built their huts on top of the rubble mound. This accidental concealment allowed Tutankhamen to lie in peace while all the other royal tombs in the valley were plundered for their riches.

Tutankhamen's tomb may have been lost, but his name was still known to Egyptologists. When all the other royal tombs had been identified, English draughtsman-turned-archaeologist

Howard Carter realized that Tutankhamen was still missing. With the support of his patron, Lord Carnarvon, he set out to strip the Valley of the Kings down to the bedrock in the search for Tutankhamen's vanished tomb.

Looking for Tutankhamen

Howard Carter (1874–1939) was an artist who became an archaeologist by accident. Living in Swaffham, Norfolk, the Carter family was acquainted with William Amherst Tyssen-Amherst, a man with a strong interest in Egyptology. When asked to recommend an artist to accompany a mission to Egypt, Amherst had no hesitation in suggesting his young neighbour. In 1891, aged 17, Howard Carter set sail for the land of the pharaohs.

In 1909 Carter met Lord Carnarvon, a wealthy man forced to winter in Egypt for his health. Carnarvon longed to excavate, but realized that he needed professional help. With Howard Carter directing, Lord Carnarvon's team discovered the tomb of Queen Hatshepsut in 1916. Inspired by this, they moved to the Valley of the Kings, where

Above: **Howard Carter was to devote the rest of his life to conserving and recording the spectacular finds discovered in Tutankhamen's tomb.**

Above: **Howard Carter used neighbouring tombs as storage centres and conservation laboratories. One tomb was even used as a dining room!**

Howard Carter began the long and expensive search for Tutankhamen.

On 1 November 1922, Carter's workmen started to excavate below the tomb of Ramesses VI. Three days later they found 16 stone steps leading to a blocked and sealed doorway. A small portion of plaster had fallen away from the upper section of the doorway, and Carter was able to peer into a corridor packed with gravel. He sent an urgent message to Lord Carnarvon:

At last have made wonderful discovery in Valley. A magnificent tomb with seals intact. Re-covered same for your arrival. Congratulations. Carter

Three weeks later Lord Carnarvon arrived, and the stairs and doorway were cleared. Soon it was possible to read the name of the occupant of the tomb: Tutankhamen. The blocked doorway was dismantled, and the corridor emptied of its fill.

The glint of gold

By 26 November Carter had found a second sealed doorway. He made a small hole, inserted a candle and peered in. To his astonishment, he could see a room packed with "strange animals, statues and gold – everywhere the glint of gold". This room, the "antechamber", held everything that Tutankhamen might need in the afterlife: beds, dismantled chariots, furniture, food and drink, flowers, and boxes filled with clothing. A second, smaller chamber – the "annex" – held even more.

The blocked and sealed entrance to the burial chamber, guarded by two life-size statues of the king, was obvious in the northern wall. But first the antechamber had to be cleared of all its treasures. On 17 February 1923, the burial chamber was officially opened in the presence of an invited audience of archaeologists and government officials. Behind the plaster wall Carter discovered a "solid wall of gold", the outermost of four concentric shrines erected around Tutankhamen's sarcophagus.

The mummy's curse?

Soon after the opening of the burial chamber, excavation was suspended for ten days, and Lord Carnarvon sailed south to enjoy a brief holiday at Aswan. Here he was bitten on the cheek by a mosquito. The bite turned septic and, although Carnarvon tried to make light of his condition, he could not fight the infection. He died in Cairo on 5 April 1923. His death caused intense and entirely unfounded speculation that there was a potent curse on Tutankhamen's tomb.

The work continues

On 12 February 1924, the cracked granite lid of Tutankhamen's sarcophagus was raised to reveal a gleaming golden coffin. In fact there were three concentric anthropoid (human-shaped) coffins, the innermost made of solid gold. Tutankhamen's mummy had been liberally coated with unguents, and was firmly stuck into this innermost coffin. With no hope of removing the body, the autopsy had to be conducted in the tomb. On 11 November 1925, two doctors, Douglas Derry and Saleh Bey Hamdi, started to unwrap the king. The results were disappointing: beneath his bandages, Tutankhamen was badly preserved.

Howard Carter spent the next decade recording the contents of Tutankhamen's tomb. Eventually his health failed and, with the full scientific publication of his work incomplete, he died in London on 2 March 1939. Today Tutankhamen lies safe and untouchable in his tomb, but archaeologists are still working on his extensive collection of grave goods.

Below left: **Tutankhamen's golden throne is decorated with a scene showing the boy king and his sister – wife Ankesenpaaten. The legs of the throne have lions' heads and claws.**

Below right: **Tutankhamen's body lay inside three concentric coffins housed in a stone sarcophagus. When the innermost coffin was opened, a stunning gold funeral mask was revealed.**

AN ANGLO-SAXON SHIP BURIAL

Sutton Hoo, England

A remarkable gravefield confirms that the Anglo-Saxons enjoyed a thriving economy and a rich culture that included elaborate burial rituals for their elite dead.

The Late Iron Age Anglo-Saxon kings of East Anglia, England, were pagans living on what was then the outer edge of the Christian world. But they were by no means uncouth, uneducated savages eking out a miserable existence in a post-Roman dark age. The gravefield discovered at Sutton Hoo, Suffolk – with its spectacular ship burial unearthed in the 1940s – offers many insights into this society, not the least of which is that these were a people capable of creating beautiful works of art.

The gravefield

The Sutton Hoo gravefield was sited on a plateau beside the estuary of the River Deben, close by the sea. Archaeological excavations show that the earliest interments were cremation burials. The ashes, dating to the mid 6th century AD, were stored in bronze bowls and buried under mounds. Later burials, dating to the early 7th century, were also covered by mounds, but were inhumations (burials of complete bodies in the earth), rather than cremations.

Eventually the gravefield housed as many as 19 or 20 burial mounds (many of which have since been almost levelled by erosion), while the flat areas between the mounds contained further burials and cremations. Many of these simpler graves housed coffinless corpses which, having been buried directly in the acidic soil, have today completely vanished, leaving behind a delicate "sand cast", or "sand-body", showing exactly where the body once lay.

A ship for a tomb

One of the latest mounds was raised for a man important enough to be buried in his own ship. (We assume a man rather than a woman on the basis of its contents.) The ship housed numerous grave goods, many of which show that England was linked to a sophisticated trade network that extended as far as the Mediterranean. There was a purse full of coins from Merovingian Gaul, a large silver dish or platter bearing the stamp of the Byzantine emperor Anastasius I (Anastasius reigned from 491–518 AD; the dish was already old when it was buried), Christian stamped bowls, Greek inscribed silver spoons, and a large "Coptic" Egyptian bronze bowl. The weaponry in the grave reveals clear stylistic and cultural links with objects found in Scandinavian burials of the same period.

This wealthy ship burial would have been relatively easy to rob. We must assume that something, a strong religious sense perhaps, prevented those who had so carefully buried their dead from re-excavating them. The Old English poem *Beowulf*, written in the 8th century AD and telling of 6th-century Scandinavian life, confirms that the belongings of the dead were not considered accessible to living men.

Whose grave?

The Anglo-Saxon kings have left us no written history. We have to rely on the 9th-century *Anglo-Saxon Chronicle*, a series of manuscripts originally compiled by monks for Alfred the Great, to learn

---

Key Facts: Sutton Hoo Ship Burial

Location: Suffolk coast, England

Date: Late Iron Age/Anglo-Saxon; the ship is dated to *c.* 624 AD

Discovered: Mound first recorded 1601; ship burial discovered 1939

Explored by: Edith Pretty, Basil Brown, and Charles Phillips

Display: The gravefield is a National Trust property open to the public; the contents of the ship burial were generously donated by Mrs Pretty to the British Museum.

Right: The partially intact iron helmet recovered from the Sutton Hoo ship burial is decorated with engraved tinned-bronze panels – a suitably impressive helmet for an Anglo-Saxon warlord.

that in 617 AD the king of Northumbria, Aethelfrith, was slain by Raedwald, king of the East Angles and high king, or overlord, of all the English kingdoms. Raedwald (599–625) belonged to the Wuffingas, a line of kings who had arrived from over the sea to unite and rule East Anglia. The exact extent of Raedwald's kingdom and influence is unknown.

Although the identity of the man in the Sutton Hoo ship burial is unknown, he was evidently a rich and powerful warrior. Many historians have speculated that the mound may have been raised for King Raedwald himself. Raedwald was undoubtedly the most important pagan figure of his era, and his 25-year reign would have given him plenty of time to prepare for an opulent funeral. It is true that he had been nominally converted to Christianity when visiting the Christian King Aethelbert of Kent, but his wife remained a pagan, and it is perhaps due to her influence that the theologically confused king raised two altars in a single temple: one altar for Christians; the other for pagans. As it turned out, his conversion was only temporary: by the end of his life Raedwald had reverted to the religion of his forebears. He would therefore have been a prime candidate for a pagan ship burial.

The first boat burial

In 1938 the Sutton Hoo gravefield lay on land owned by Edith Pretty, a wealthy landowner who had developed an interest in archaeology after a visit to Egypt. Her estate contained several earth mounds, one of which had been excavated in 1863 and yielded six bushels of iron nails, which had been given to the local blacksmith. When she decided to investigate the other round mounds, she approached local archaeologist Basil Brown for help. Assisted by Mrs Pretty's gardener, John Jacobs, and her gamekeeper, William Spooner, the digging team spent its first season on the site investigating three of the smaller mounds (known as Mounds 2, 3, and 4). They discovered a series of cremations which had been robbed and, in Mound 2, a handful of iron rivets which Brown, perhaps remembering that the remains of an Anglo-Saxon ship burial had been found at nearby Snape in 1862, correctly identified as parts of a wooden boat.

The vanished ship

The following year the team decided to tackle a larger mound (Mound 1). Just two days into the excavation they discovered an iron rivet; a few hours later a ship started to emerge from the soil. The ship's timber had decayed, but a thin "cast" of hard sand, and rows of iron rivets still in their original position, preserved its shape perfectly.

The ship was an open rowing boat some 27 m (88 ft) long with a large steering paddle on the starboard side of the hull. There was no evidence of a mast, and experts estimate that the ship would have required a crew of 40 oarsmen. Areas of patching and repair showed that the ship had been used before its burial. A large timber-framed room, built in the centre of the ship, served as the burial chamber

On learning of the discovery a team of experts descended on Sutton Hoo, led by Charles Philips of Cambridge University. They had to work quickly; World War II was looming, threatening to bring an end to all British excavations. The ship was emptied of its treasures, then surveyed and photographed by the Science Museum in August 1939; these official photographic records would be lost during the conflict with Germany. Fortunately two amateur photographers, Barbara Wagstaff and Mercie Lack, had been allowed to

take many hundreds of photographs of the ship, and their records were available to help archaeologists after the war determine what the ship had originally looked like. Meanwhile the precious finds were stored for safety in a tunnel at London's Aldwych Underground station.

Conservation of the finds started in 1946 under the supervision of Rupert Bruce-Mitford of the British Museum. There would be further excavations at Sutton Hoo between 1965 and 1970, when a plaster cast was taken of the now sadly deteriorated boat, and between 1983 and 1992. Excavations in 2000 revealed the presence of an earlier cemetery.

The body and its goods

Despite scrupulous excavation, no trace of a body was found. This, and the lack of intimate personal possessions, led to suggestions that there never had been a body – perhaps the ship was a cenotaph (an empty tomb)? But, as a series of iron fittings appears to mark the position of a vanished rectangular coffin, it seems more likely that the corpse simply dissolved in the damp and highly acid soil. This theory was confirmed in 1967 when scientific analysis of the soil in the burial chamber revealed an unusually high level of phosphates, a group of chemicals released by decaying bodies.

Fortunately many of the grave goods, stored in the central chamber, were more or less intact. These included a range of coins, a complete set of weapons, musical instruments, textiles and leather garments, a set of buckets and cauldrons, and gold, silver, and bronze artefacts of remarkable craftsmanship. The most magnificent object is a partially intact iron helmet and facemask decorated with engraved tinned-bronze panels showing mythological scenes. This, one of only four known Anglo-Saxon helmets, was in pieces when it was discovered, leading to speculation that it might have been destroyed deliberately on the death of its owner.

Above: **The sand cast left by the decayed Sutton Hoo burial ship has allowed archaeologists to reconstruct the vanished boat. No trace of a body was found inside the sand cast.**

3

CITIES & DWELLING PLACES

The earliest archaeologists set out to make
spectacular discoveries. With little interest in the
humdrum existence of ordinary people, they
focused their energies on long-lost temples and
hopefully gold-filled tombs built by the ancient
elite. Today's archaeologists see things very
differently, and have developed a deep interest in
investigating both how and where the ancients
chose to live. They realize that it is only by
excavating dwelling places – be they tents, simple
stone huts, or magnificent mud-brick palaces in
extensive cities – that we can start to gain a
proper understanding of daily life for both rich
and poor in the ancient world.

The earliest humans were hunter-gatherers who lived in small, nomadic or semi-nomadic bands, and spent their days following the food that served as their mobile larder. They had relatively few possessions, and it is not surprising that their dwelling places are difficult for today's archaeologists to locate. Sites such as Dolní Vestonice, in the Czech Republic, offer us a rare glimpse of domestic life during the Palaeolithic, or Old Stone Age.

When humans ceased to be full-time nomadic big game hunters they began to live in permanent, year-round settlements, and built substantial dwelling places. Now there was no limit to the number of possessions that an individual could own and store, and some lucky, or astute, families started to accrue far more wealth than others. For the poorest members of the community, city life was not necessarily an improvement on the hunter-gatherer existence. Settled families tend to be larger than nomadic families, and increasing family size reduced female life expectancy as more women and babies died in childbirth. Large numbers of people living in cramped housing saw increased risk from pests and diseases, while the obvious differences in personal wealth – rich and poor living in close proximity – encouraged the development of crime.

The newly rich patrons could afford to support the artists and craftsmen working in the new industries that now began to emerge. These included the mass production of pottery and glass. Soon complex societies developed, with a wealthy and politically empowered elite supported by a relatively poor and unimportant non-elite. The traces of these varied lives, rich and poor, craftsmen and kings, are preserved in the ruins of their houses, towns, and cities.

The excavation of a town or city site is technically difficult, time-consuming, and expensive. Some settlements – Pompeii and Herculaneum, Italy, being perhaps the most famous examples – were abandoned suddenly and never reoccupied; they present the archaeologist with a snapshot of abruptly truncated life on one particular day in the ancient world. But long-lasting settlements tend to have phases of buildings tiered one on top of another. In the Near East this repeated building led to the formation of tells, large mud-brick mounds made from collapsed mud-brick housing. To reach the bottom – or oldest – levels, it is of course necessary for the archaeologist to cut down through the more recent levels, each of which has to be properly recorded. The situation becomes even more complicated where there is a modern town or building covering all or part of an ancient site, or when, as at Alexandria, Egypt, part of the city has been submerged beneath the sea.

Yet the difficulties of excavating a residential site – be it a hamlet or a city – are more than outweighed by the exciting and rewarding aspects of archaeology. Ancient dwelling sites offer us the chance to study not only the elite, but also the humbler members of society; the workers, the women, the elderly, and the children who are so often overlooked in written histories.

The first archaeologists to excavate occupation sites worked on a grand scale, employing large gangs of unskilled labourers to clear vast areas each season. They paid particular attention to the elite architecture – the palaces and temples – while rushing through the housing and workshops occupied by the poorer classes. All too often their work was ill conserved, and is effectively lost to us. Today we have a greater awareness that archaeologists must study society as a whole, from the highest emperor to the lowliest servant. We do not just want to find precious objects to display in our museums; we want to find an understanding of the past – and that understanding has to include an appreciation of how things were made, who made them, and how and why they were used. This means that archaeologists now work on a much smaller scale, collecting and analyzing every single scrap of evidence, including domestic rubbish and animal dung. Back in the lab, a humble scrap of linen or a single grain of wheat can yield valuable information about long-lost ways of life.

SETTLING DOWN
Dolní Vestonice, Czech Republic

The remains of a small Central European settlement tell us much about the beginnings of settled life 27,000 years ago.

People lived in the Pavlov hills of Moravia in the Czech Republic throughout prehistory. By far the most important site in this region is the Gravettian (mid-Upper Palaeolithic) open-air site of Dolní Vestonice, which was first excavated by Czech archaeologist Karel Absolon in the mid 1920s, and later by Bohuslav Klima. It is of world importance not only for the impressive extent of its remains of open-air dwellings and workshops, but also for its remarkable evidence of very early textiles and terracottas, its quantity of art objects, and its fascinating burials.

Huts and bones

Located almost 300 km (186 miles) southeast of Prague, Dolní Vestonice lies on a sloping terrace of the River Dyje, with its lower part on a swampy area with a stream. Next to this depression, which contained an abundance of mammoth bones, were tent-like huts, each with two hearths. A huge central hearth, covering nearly 3 sq m (3½ sq yd), was also unearthed there. It contained more than a thousand tools and flakes, indicating that it was a work area.

One large hut measured 9 x 15 m (39 x 49 ft) and contained five small hearths, each about 1 m (just over 3 ft) in diameter. It probably had walls of animal skins supported by a framework of stone and posts. Inside were numerous artefacts, and outside was a large pile of bones, the remains of an estimated 100 mammoths, mostly young, which had presumably been used as fuel as well as raw material and weights for walls.

Around the settlement area were further accumulations of mammoth bones, some apparently stored to serve as building materials and others as fuel. In other areas there were tusks stuck into the ground to form slight walls, which provided a kind of boundary. Other bone piles and heavy stone tools near the stream seemed to be the areas where animals had been butchered and prepared.

Higher up the slope than the rest of the huts was a circular structure, about 6 m (20 ft) in diameter, known as Dolní Vestonice II, discovered in 1951. It had a retaining wall of limestone blocks that had supported roof posts. As the large post holes were located on only one side of the circle, it seems that the roof must have sloped down to the ground. Inside this hut, there were only a few bones and tools, but in the centre was a kind of oval hearth edged with blackened clay made of soil mixed with ground limestone, enclosing a dug-out hearth containing soot and more than 2000 lumps of fired clay. This feature is thought to be a kiln of some kind.

Works of art or ritual?

The site became renowned for its terracottas which, together with those from similar sites nearby such as Pavlov to the southeast, are among the oldest known artefacts of their kind in the world. They comprise small figurines of animals and a few humans, and display some spatial differentiation – herbivores in one hut, for example, and human figurines in the centre of

Key Facts: Dolní Vestonice	
Location: Pavlov Hills, Moravia, Czech Republic	**Explored by:** Karel Absolon, 1924–38; Bohuslav Klíma in the 1940s and 1970s
Date: Palaeolithic, 27–24,000 BC	
Discovered: Bones and stone tools found by local scholars from 1911 onward	**Display:** Nothing to see at the site; finds at the Moravian Museum, Brno, Czech Republic

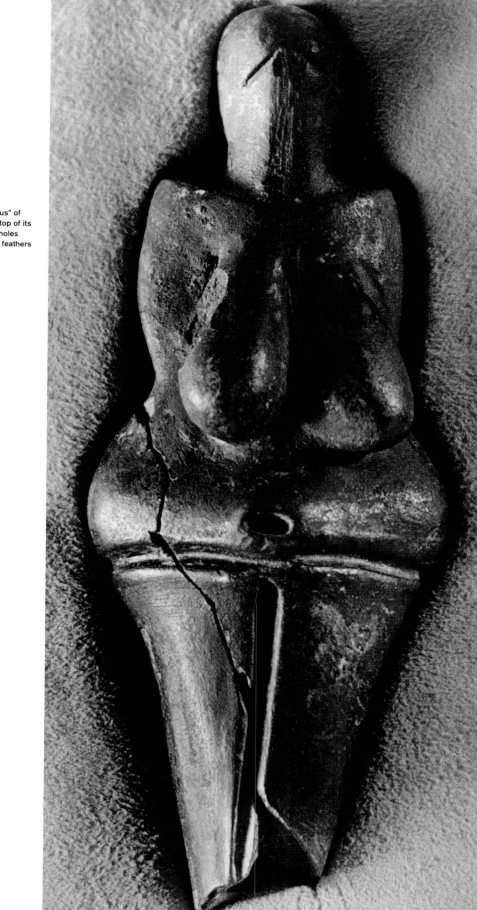

Right: **The black "Venus" of Dolní Vestonice. The top of its head contains small holes which may have held feathers or plants.**

Above: The enigmatic triple burial of Dolní Vestonice found in 1986; opinions are still strongly divided about the sex of the central skeleton, and the scenario that may lie behind this discovery.

another, together with carnivores. These works of art were all made by firing wetted loess, a loamy deposit of clay, sand, and animal and vegetable matter. The same technique was applied to the most famous of the site's figurines – the black "Venus", 11.4 cm (4½ in) long, which was found in the settlement's central fireplace. Its head has two slits for eyes, and the body is wide, with long and pendulous breasts. There is a horizontal groove at the junction of legs and body, and paired grooves also extend across the back.

Fingerprints have even survived on fired loess from the site. Tests on some figurines indicate that they were fired at temperatures of 500°–800°C (900°–1500°F), and the shape of their fractures implies that they were broken by thermal shock – they must have been placed, while still wet, in the hottest part of the fire, and thus deliberately caused to explode. So, rather than carefully made art objects, their lack of finish and the manner of their breakage suggest that they may have been used in some special ritual. Of the site's 77 miniature animal figurines in good condition, carnivorous species predominate: there are 21 bears, 9 lions, 5 wolves, and 3 foxes.

Some of the fired clay found at this site and at Pavlov has impressions of textiles or flexible basketry – the oldest surviving traces of this technology in the world. Work in textiles and cordage during the period was clearly sophisticated, diverse, and widespread.

A small settlement

Dolní Vestonice was originally seen as a mammoth hunters' camp, but today it is doubted that mammoths were hunted very frequently, and it is now thought that mammoth bones were simply collected over long periods of time from carcasses and skeletons encountered in the region. Later excavations at the site produced radiocarbon dates which placed it around 27,000–24,000 years ago. It has been estimated that each of the five or six structures might have housed a family unit of about 20 people, thus suggesting a population of more than 100.

Dolní Vestonice also yielded tens of thousands of flint tools, and numerous bone implements, such as points, spatulae and wands, and antler shovels; the site is also known for a wealth of tools and carvings in mammoth ivory. For

Left: **Two mammoth-ivory carvings from the site, both of which are thought by some scholars to be stylized representations of women. The engraved rod on the left with its carved breasts (or perhaps testicles?) is 8.7 cm (3.4 in) long. The forked pendant on very slightly smaller.**

example, a spoon was decorated with an intricate geometric motif. A series of tiny ivory pendants, only about 2.5 cm (1 in) high, may represent stylized breasts or testicles. By far the most famous ivory carving from the site, however, was a thumb-sized head, 4.8 cm (2 in) long, found in 1936, which seems to be that of a woman; at any rate it has an elaborate coiffure. The asymmetry of its face has led some people to link it with an enigmatic individual in the centre of a remarkable triple burial.

An enigmatic burial

Several burials were found around the site; these included the grave of a woman covered by two mammoth bones – a scapula and part of a pelvis. In 1986 excavation uncovered a shallow pit containing three skeletons, lying side by side. All three people were young, between 17 and 20 years of age. The eldest, lying on its back in the centre, was gracefully slender, and this, together with the shape of the pelvis, points to a female. On her left was the big robust skeleton of a male, 1.75 m (5 ft 9 in) tall, lying on his stomach with his head turned away from her. His left arm covered the

female's hand. On her right was a smaller robust male, aged 18 or 19, lying on his left side and facing the female. Both of his arms touched her pelvis. The grave also contained a quantity of red ochre, some ivory beads, and perforated animal teeth. Some fragments of carbonized wood on and around the skeletons may be the remains of some kind of tomb cover, and produced a radiocarbon date of 26,640 years ago.

The skeletons had clearly been buried at about the same time, with the female having been put in first. Her bones show signs of several pathological deformations. She had an asymmetrical skull, scoliosis of the spine, deformation of the pelvis, and an insufficient development of her entire right side and limbs. These symptoms all suggest that she had contracted rickets or encephalitis at an early age. The male with his hand on her pelvis was skewered by a large piece of wood, while the other male's skull was smashed. It is possible that these two apparently healthy and powerful males were sacrificed to accompany the dead female, but some specialists remain unconvinced that the central figure is indeed a female rather than an effeminate male.

A SOPHISTICATED CITY
Çatal Hüyük, Turkey

Nine thousand years ago, Çatal Hüyük, one of the world's first cities, flourished on the Konya Plain in south-central Turkey.

The city of Çatal Hüyük (literally "Fork" or "Twin Mound") covered 13 hectares (32 acres), stood 17 m (55 ft) above the marshy Konya Plain, had at least 14 distinct occupation levels, and was home to perhaps as many as 10,000 inhabitants who lived in a closely packed mass of honeycomb-like mud-brick housing built with timber posts. There were few streets or alleyways at Çatal Hüyük. The houses had no doors, and were entered via their flat roofs, using ladders. This system may seem strange today, but it would have ensured that the rooms remained cool in the hot Turkish summers and warm in the cold winters.

"Shrines" and burials

Religion was an important part of daily life. Some of the decorated rooms in the housing complex were originally thought to have been shrines; these dwellings have plastered and colourfully painted walls decorated with what we assume to be religious murals. They show detailed hunting rituals featuring large animals, vultures with human-looking legs, a repeated leopard motif, and abstract geometric patterning. The rooms have also yielded bulls' horns, bulls' heads, and human skulls displayed on platforms or benches, while a series of baked clay figurines, generally identified as "mother goddesses" or fertility figurines, shows a variety of plump women, including women in childbirth.

Originally these scenes were interpreted in a very literal way, and it was assumed that priests, perhaps dressed in vulture costumes, used the shrines for ritual purposes. However, recent microscopic analysis of the refuse which litters the floors of the "shrines" has shown that it is simple domestic rubbish; it seems that at Çatal Hüyük the distinction between the secular and the sacred was not clear cut.

The dead of Çatal Hüyük were buried in family vaults beneath the floors of their decorated houses. Often their bodies were defleshed before burial; their bare bones were then tied together and sprinkled with red-ochre pigment. Some of the wealthier citizens were buried with grave goods of copper, turquoise, and seashells. Some graves included curious polished obsidian hemispheres which archaeologist James Mellaart interpreted as mirrors. One grave, discovered in the 1960s, yielded an unusual flint knife, its handle in the shape of a snake. A second flint knife, its bone handle carved into the shape of a wild boar's head, was found in a small building almost 40 years later. Flint was both rare and precious at Çatal Hüyük, and most of the edge tools were made from obsidian, which was obtained from the volcanic peaks to the northeast of the city.

Hacilar

The discovery of such a large and obviously successful community outside the Fertile Crescent (the curve of land stretching across Mesopotamia, Syria, and Palestine, where agriculture first developed) greatly surprised archaeologists, who wondered exactly why such a sophisticated city

Key Facts: Çatal Hüyük

Location: The Konya Plain, south-central Turkey

Date: Neolithic: *c.* 7000–5000 BC

Discovered: By British archaeologist James Mellaart in the 1950s; first excavated in 1961

Explored by: James Mellaart in the early 1960s; a more resent survey, excavation, and conservation project, scheduled to last from 1993–2018, is led by Ian Hodder

Display: The site is open to the public, but access to some areas may be restricted. A visitors' centre is planned

should have flourished in splendid isolation on this particular spot, at this time. However, more recent excavations in Turkey have revealed that Çatal Hüyük was not, as had initially been assumed, the only substantial Neolithic settlement in the area.

In southwestern Turkey, on the northern side of the Taurus Mountain range, lies the city mound of Hacilar. The earliest phase of the city, which dates to before 7000 BC, belongs to the pre-pottery Neolithic. The site was then deserted, before being reoccupied in the late Neolithic– early Chalcolithic (copper age), c. 5600–4500 BC. The people of this later city built mud-brick, closely packed houses on stone foundations. Their houses had flat roofs; stairways suggest that the roofs may have served as additional open-air rooms. The

most important artefact to come from Hacilar is the distinctive hand-made pottery that includes vessels, and statuettes of the "mother goddesses". Plant remains indicate that the people of Hacilar practised agriculture at an early date, with cereals and pulses forming an important part of their diet.

Archaeologists set to work

In the late 1950s British archaeologist James Mellaart, of the Institute of Archaeology, London University, was conducting a survey of archaeological sites in central Turkey when he discovered the twin mounds of Çatal Hüyük. He returned to excavate in 1961, and was amazed by what he found. In just four seasons he uncovered more than 150 buildings, and an astonishing collection of art and religious material including an

Above: **The great Neolithic cities of the Near East were built of mud brick, taken from the fertile land from which they sprang. Mud brick eventually corrodes to form** *tell* **sites: raised archaeological mounds.**

impressive series of murals, Çatal Hüyük was the first substantial Neolithic site to be found in Anatolia, and Mellaart's work forced archaeologists to reconsider their understanding of the development of agriculture and early settlements during the Neolithic phase in the Near East.

In 1965 Mellaart's team realized that it was not possible to adequately conserve the painted plaster walls, so work at Çatal Hüyük came to a halt. Less than 5 per cent of the site had been uncovered, and the deepest levels were still untouched. Many of the plaster murals had already been detached from their mud-brick walls, either by removing both the plaster and the mud-brick wall together, or by sticking the plaster to linen cloth, then peeling it away from the wall. The wall paintings were transferred to the Museum of Anatolian Civilization in Ankara, where they are now displayed.

Later excavations

Work at the site started again in 1993, under Ian Hodder of Stanford University, USA. In the intervening 30 years technological advances had transformed the practice of archaeology, and as a result the new team's methods were quite unlike those of Mellaaart.

The latest excavations are being carried out by a multidisciplinary team that takes a conservation-based approach to the site; the removal of a mural from its original context would now be undertaken only if it were absolutely essential to do so – in other words, only if the archaeologists are sure that it would be destroyed if it were left in situ. As merely exposing the ancient plaster to the environment causes it to dry out and crack, the new team has started a long-term mural conservation project under the leadership of Frank Matero of the Architectural Conservation Laboratory at the University of Pennsylvania, USA. One of its most successful conservation treatments has been the injection of liquid mortar grout into the walls;

this has been effective in reattaching fallen pieces of plaster.

A robust economy

The people of Çatal Hüyük were farmers who irrigated their fields, cultivated wheat and barley, kept domesticated sheep and goats, and hunted wild cattle, horses, and deer. They were some of the first peoples to use lead and copper to make jewellery, and they traded extensively in obsidian. Çatal Hüyük pottery was initially rather crude, although it developed over time, but the weavers produced accomplished work in both linen and wool. Finished fabrics were stamped with colourful dyes using pottery stamp seals.

Mellaart assumed, on the basis of the bull-decorated "shrines", that meat at Çatal Hüyük came from cattle. But recent analysis of fragments of animal bones recovered by soil sieving has shown that the inhabitants of Çatal Hüyük ate large quantities of sheep and goat. Meanwhile soil analysis, now standard archaeological procedure, has led to the discovery of large amounts of animal dung within the housing mass, and it is now known that some of the domestic "courtyards" identified by Mellaart's team were actually animal pens used to shelter the sheep and goats during the snowy winter months.

Plant remains reveal more about the Çatal Hüyük diet, which was rich in fruits, cereals, legumes, and nuts including acorns, pistachios, and almonds. At first, the people gathered most of their plant food, but as they gradually progressed they cultivated it themselves. Scirpus reeds, gathered from nearby marshes, were particularly useful; they yielded rhizomes that could be eaten either fresh or dried, and stalks that could be woven into baskets, roofing, and clothing.

As yet there is no obvious reason why such a thriving site should have been abandoned; it may simply be that its marshy location was just too far away from the trade routes that were starting to criss cross the Near East.

Right: Religion was an important part of daily life at Çatal Hüyük. The meaning of much of the art of the Neolithic is obscure, but is assumed to have had some religious meaning.

A PREHISTORIC VILLAGE
Skara Brae, Scotland

Stone huts with built-in furniture and indoor toilets are among the features that characterize Skara Brae, the best-preserved prehistoric village in northern Europe.

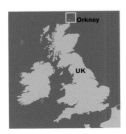

Skara Brae is located on the coast of mainland Orkney, an island to the north of Scotland. This semi-subterranean settlement came to light when a severe storm in 1850 stripped grass from a sand dune and exposed a huge refuse heap and the ruins of a cluster of ancient stone houses. Important excavations were carried out here in the late 1920s, and more recently in the 1970s.

Skara Brae was inhabited continuously for about 600 years, between *c.* 3100 and 2500 BC. The village that can be seen today dates primarily from the latter part of that period, when it was decided to improve the living conditions and build larger houses than those of the original village. Some of the latter structures are still visible.

Well-appointed homes

The stone houses have a quite spacious floor area of about 36 sq m (43 sq yd) and feature a typically narrow door, which helped to keep out the winds. The door was a slab of stone or wood. It is assumed that the roofs, now vanished, were made of wood and turf, and rested on beams of timber or whale bone.

The furniture in the houses is made largely of stone, presumably because it was durable, and there were almost no large trees on Orkney. Moreover, the local flagstone was readily available, easy to work, and was an ideal construction material. Opposite the doors stand dressers for the storage and display of objects. Set into the floor are small watertight tanks, thought to be for soaking limpets to be used as fish bait. There is

also a large grinding stone. The fireplace is in the centre, and there is a stone seat between the dresser and the hearth. As no charcoal has been found, it is clear that wood was not burned here – instead the fuel must have been animal dung, dried seaweed, heather, bracken, and oil-rich bones from marine animals such as whales.

Bedding and plumbing

At either side of the house are box beds, with more storage spaces in the walls above, and there are also cells or alcoves set into the thickness of the walls. In some houses, the beds themselves were also built into the walls. Presumably the bedding was made of bracken, sheepskin, and other animal hides. There is evidence from drains that some houses may have had indoor toilets. In some of the house walls and passages there are enigmatic geometric motifs incised into stones.

Between the dwellings, passages roofed with stone slabs ran through the midden (refuse mound) of ash, shells, bones, and other waste into which they were built and which protected them from the elements.

Overall, this seems a quite sophisticated set of structures, with a notion of privacy, as each dwelling seems to have been a house for a family rather than communal. The people – probably about 20 families living together – grew cereals; traces of these have been found, and cultivation was doubtless made possible by the fact that during the period of occupation the temperature was probably slightly higher than it is today. They

---

Key Facts: Skara Brae

Location: Mainland Orkney, Scotland

Date: Neolithic, 3100–2500 BC

Discovered: 1850

Explored by: V. Gordon Childe 1927–30 and D. Clarke in 1972–3

Display: The site is open to the public; finds can be seen at Orkney Museum (Kirkwall) and National Museum of Scotland (Edinburgh)

also kept cattle and a few pigs, as well as sheep and goats. Naturally, an abundance of fish bones has also been recovered, mainly cod and saithe.

Tools and jewellery

Tools were made of flint, poor local chert, and bones. A number of strangely carved stone objects has been unearthed, which may have been used in religious rites. Jewellery comprised beads, pendants, and pins, almost all made of bone, but colour may also have been used in ornament-ation, as "paint pots" of shell, bone, and stone have been found to contain red ochre.

After the village was abandoned – for reasons unknown – sand filled and covered it, and also helped to preserve it. Similar sites in the Orkneys include Rinyo and Noltland.

Above: **House 1** in the village shows the basic layout, with the stone dresser, the two beds at either side of the central hearth, the small fish tanks in the floor, and the grinding stones.

THE PALACE OF KNOSSOS
Herakleion, Crete

A wealthy, complex society arose on the island of Crete in the Bronze Age – a society epitomized by the sophisticated palace complex at Knossos.

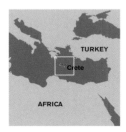

According to legend, King Minos was an ancient ruler of the Mediterranean island of Crete. Beneath his splendid palace at Knossos was a maze in which he kept the Minotaur, a vicious creature that was half-man, half-bull. Eventually the Minotaur was defeated by the Greek hero Theseus with the help of the beautiful princess Ariadne. When British archaeologist Arthur Evans (1851–1941) needed a name for the distinctive Bronze Age civilization which he was uncovering in the remains of the Knossos palace, he remembered the story of King Minos, and the Minoan period was born.

Minoan society

As islanders, Minoans naturally developed their own distinctive architecture, art, and traditions. But they were by no means an isolated community. They participated fully in the flourishing Mediterranean trade networks, importing copper and tin to make bronze, and exporting a range of commodities, including olive oil. Their fertile land made them a secure and wealthy people. Cereals, olives, and vines all flourished, while the terrain was well suited to the raising of sheep and goats. This wealth was translated into ambitious building projects, which were made possible by the plentiful supplies of wood and stone.

Bronze Age Crete was a stratified society in which a minority of families controlled the island's wealth. Not everyone was literate. The earliest palace-based administrators used two forms of writing, known today as Cretan Hieroglyphic script and Linear A. At Knossos, Linear B, an early form of Greek, eventually superseded Linear A. While Hieroglyphic script was used mainly on seal stones, Linear A and B were used to record temporary documents on unbaked clay tablets. Fortunately, some of these tablets were preserved by having been accidentally baked in fires that destroyed other parts of the archives. Linear B was decoded by Michael Ventris in 1952, but the earlier scripts remain undeciphered. The Minoan writings that we can read are essentially accounting and administrative records: so, as we have no written Minoan history, our understanding of the Minoan way of life is firmly rooted in archaeology.

First and Second palaces

Evans used the experience of his own discoveries at Knossos to divide the Minoan period into three chronological phases, each with three subdivisions: early (*c.* 3000–2000 BC), middle (*c.* 2000–1550 BC), and late (*c.* 1550–1050 BC). His scheme is now regarded as oversimplistic, but is retained for convenience in many published works. Today many archaeologists prefer to classify Minoan development on the basis of architectural development.

The First Palaces were built at Knossos, Phaistos, and Mallia (and possibly at Chania and Zakros) around 1950 BC. These were destroyed by a series of earthquakes two and a half centuries later. They were rebuilt on a far grander scale and,

Key Facts: Knossos

Location: Near modern Herakleion, Crete

Date: Minoan (Bronze Age), c. 1950–1375 BC

Discovered: First recognized by Minos Kalokairinos in 1878

Explored by: Excavated by Arthur Evans

Display: The Palace is open to the public; artefacts from the site are displayed in the Herakleion Museum and in the Ashmolean Museum, Oxford.

despite the eruption of the voclanic Mount Thera in about 1530 BC, the Second Palaces flourished until around 1450 BC, when almost all the palaces – Knossos excepted – were destroyed probably by Mycenaean invaders from the Greek mainland. Knossos survived until *c.* 1375 BC, by which time it, too, was under Mycenaean control.

Knosssos

The Minoan palaces were not simply the ancient equivalent of our modern royal residences. They did include accommodation, but they were also political, administrative, and religious centres equipped with substantial storage facilities for agricultural produce, and well-stocked workshops employing a variety of craft specialists. Each palace was effective within a given region or territory, but from the beginning Knossos, standing on a low hill in the valley of the Kairatos River, almost 6 km (4 miles) inland from Crete's northern coast, was the largest and most architecturally complex of all. Built around a

Above: **The sea was of crucial importance to the Minoans, as reflected in this dolphin fresco from the palace of Knossos.**

large central court, the palace of Knossos included a warren of rooms on several levels, many decorated with fine wall paintings. Outside the palace was a substantial and prosperous unfortified town that, at its peak, may have had as many as 20,000 inhabitants. Whoever controlled Knossos effectively controlled Crete. When, in 1375 BC, the palace was finally destroyed by fire, Knossos retained its importance, becoming one of the most prominent Cretan Greek cities.

Arthur Evans

Arthur Evans was the son of Sir John Evans, a distinguished prehistorian who achieved worldwide recognition for his work on early European stone tools. After a period working as foreign correspondent for the *Manchester Guardian*, in 1884 Arthur Evans took up a less demanding position as curator of the Ashmolean Museum, Oxford. Having developed a keen interest in early Greek seal stones, many of which came from Crete, he visited the island and was

shown the neglected site of Knossos. Knossos had already been the subject of one brief archaeological mission. In 1878 Minos Kalokairinos had excavated one of the palace storerooms, and discovered an array of storage jars. Nine years later, visiting archaeologist Heinrich Schliemann had determined to buy the site with a view to excavating it; however, when negotiations with the Turkish landowner broke down, Schliemann returned to Troy and Knossos was left untouched.

Now Evans, too, determined to buy the site. After a protracted period of negotiations he succeeded, and began work on 23 March 1900. Within a week he found an inscribed clay tablet proving, as he had always suspected, that the early Cretans were literate. By 10 April 1900 he had started to uncover the first of many frescoes. Knossos was to become his lifetime's work.

Inside the palaces

The First Palace of Knossos had been built on the levelled remains of a Neolithic settlement. Today it is mainly hidden beneath the later Second Palace, but we know that it was originally an imposing multipurpose building with a central court, storage facilities, and workshops.

The Second Palace also had a large, rectangular central court, plentiful storage facilities, and ceremonial and living accommodation. However, Evan's habit of naming and ascribing functions to rooms – for example, "The Domestic Quarters", "The Hall of the Double-Axes" (interpreted by Evans as the king's room), and the connecting "Queen's Megaron" (private quarters) – can sometimes lead to confusion. It is not always possible to assign a precise, single purpose to a given room, although in the case of the Queen's Megaron it seems that Evans may have been correct. This room, decorated with an accomplished dolphin frieze, has a small en suite

Left: Arthur Evans did not just excavate at Knossos, but also reconstructed much of the ancient city as he imagined it to have looked.

bathroom including a bath (now broken) and a toilet that hint at private use. Evans also identified a beautifully decorated "Throne Room" complex, complete with a lustral basin, although his imposing gypsum "throne" was probably nothing of the kind. Archaeologists now regard the "Throne Room" as one of a group of small shrines on the west side of the Central Court.

Decoration

The Knossos palace is famous for its frescoed walls. In Crete, the basic fresco technique had developed by the end of the Neolithic period, although the full palette of mineral-based pigments did not emerge until the First Palace period, when the artists had red, yellow, white, grey, and blue at their disposal. The earliest frescoes, painted onto smooth lime plaster, were either geometric designs or scenes taken from nature. The first figured fresco is the "Saffron Gatherer" found at Knossos; this was most unfortunately "restored" to show the image of a

boy, and only recently corrected to show the blue monkey (probably grey in real life) that the ancient artist intended. By convention, in the later scenes, males were painted a red-brown colour, females were white, and plants and vegetation were often blue.

Bull-leaping

Bull-leaping frescoes – scenes that show both male and female acrobats (the females identified by their skin colour) vaulting over the backs of large bulls – are often interpreted as religious rituals rather than simple sports. Bull-leaping was certainly an important aspect of Minoan life; it is also found in small-scale statuary, and was exported by Minoan fresco painters to the Egyptian Delta palace of Avaris. Two other important statues, recovered from the Knossos "Temple Repositories", show a bare-breasted "snake goddess", either holding two writhing snakes at arm's length, or with serpents twisting around her arms.

NEBUCHADNEZZAR'S CAPITAL

Babylon, Iraq

King Nebuchadnezzar transformed the ancient capital of Babylonia into the most dazzling city in the Mesopotamian world.

Babylon, the capital of ancient Babylonia, stood on either side of a branch of the Euphrates River, some 96 km (60 miles) to the southwest of Baghdad in modern Iraq. Babylon has had a long and turbulent history, with successive phases of building and destruction. Its archaeology is correspondingly complex. The main city site, the Babylon preserved in the works of the classical writers, is the Babylon built by King Nebuchadnezzar in the 6th century BC.

Early history

Most of the lower levels of Babylon are now lost beneath the high water table. As a result of this and later destruction, we have only a scanty understanding of the earliest phases of the city's development – the Akkadian (*c.* 2330–2150 BC) and Old Babylonian (*c.* 2000–1600 BC) phases.

Cuneiform writings confirm that Babylon was for a time the capital city of King Sargon of Akkad (*c.* 2330–2280 BC). At this stage, the city is known to have had at least two temples. After its initial flourishing, Babylon shrank to the status of a small town until the reign of King Hammurabi (1792–1750 BC). Hammurabi succeeded in uniting Babylonia and neighbouring Assyria; his new kingdom quickly became immensely wealthy, and that wealth was used to fund a building programme at Babylon. This included the construction of city walls and gateways, and of numerous shrines including a splendid new temple dedicated to the principal deity, Marduk (called Bel by the Greeks). Hammurabi is today remembered for the code of laws that he designed to be applied throughout his territories.

Hammurabi's hard-won kingdom did not long survive his death. Eventually Babylon fell to the Assyrians, and was occupied for more than a century. The Assyrians added to the building works, but resistance to Assyrian domination ran high. In 689 BC, in an act of gross sacrilege, the Assyrian king Sennacherib had the temples flattened. Sennacherib was subsequently murdered – his death was seen by many as the gods' revenge – and his successor Esarhaddon rebuilt Babylon.

The Assyrian empire eventually collapsed. This allowed King Nabopolassar of the Neo-Babylonian dynasty (625–605 BC) to force his way into Assyrian-held territories. Nabopolassar was succeeded by his son, Nebuchadnezzar (605–562 BC), a charismatic and successful general who oversaw the development of Babylon into a city that reflected the empire's power and wealth.

The Hanging Gardens and Tower of Babel

Classical authors tell us that King Nebuchadnezzar built the fabulous Hanging Gardens of Babylon to please his wife Amyitis, who was homesick for the mountainous region to the east of Babylonia in which she had been brought up. These gardens, which were reportedly supported on stone columns and which were artificially irrigated, quickly became immortalized in the works of the classical authors as one of the Seven Wonders of the Ancient World. According to the 1st-century

Key Facts: Babylon	
Location: Southern Iraq	**Explored by:** Deutsche Orientgesellschaft, directed by Robert Koldewey, 1899–1917
Date: Continuous occupation from *c.* 2330 BC; the Neo-Babylonian city dates to the 1st millennium BC	**Display:** The site is currently inaccessible. Many earlier finds are now housed in the Baghdad Museum. The Ishtar Gate is in the Pergamonmuseum, Berlin
Discovered: Never lost	

Greek writer Strabo, the Hanging Gardens of Babylon were situated on the banks of the Euphrates, but there is no trace of them there today: they are entirely lost. Although archaeologist Robert Koldewey had tentatively identified a group of underground rooms, apparently waterproofed with asphalt, in Nebuchadnezzar's palace as a possible location, many archaeologists now believe that the Hanging Gardens were actually situated in the contemporary city of Nineveh.

The Biblical story of the Tower of Babel (found in Genesis 11:3–4) also belongs to the time of King Nebuchadnezzar:

And they said one to another Go to, let us make brick, and burn them thoroughly. And they had brick for stone, and slime had they for mortar.

And they said Go to, let us build us a city and a tower, whose top may reach unto heaven …

The tower is understood to have been a ziggurat, or stepped mud-brick temple.

Nebuchadnezzar conquered much of the Levant, including Jerusalem, and captured many Jews whom he took back with him to Babylon. Babylon therefore features in Jewish history as a city of oppression and fear, where Daniel would read the writing on the wall.

Babylon in later times

The mud-brick mounds of Babylon were never lost, and never forgotten. Ancient Greek tourists, including Herodotus, the historian of the 5th century BC, recorded their visits to the site, and early Arab and European travellers stood and

Above: The artistic skills of the ancient sculptors is revealed in this scene showing King Ur-Nammu making an offering to the moon god Nannar.

Above: **The excavation of the ancient palace involved digging a trench 12.2 m (40 ft) deep and several hundred feet long, cutting through the many occupation levels of the ancient city of Babylon.**

Right: **The magnificent Ishtar Gate, built by King Nebuchadnezzar, allowed access to the inner city. It was decorated with a series of imposing animals**

marvelled before the thick mud-brick walls. In 1650 Pietro della Valle attempted to identify the remains of the Tower of Babel in the mud-brick ruins to the north of the site. But Babylon would not be formally investigated until the late 19th century, when a team from the Deutsche Orientgesellschaft, directed by archaeologist Robert Koldewey, started excavations in 1899. By this time, the ruins at Nineveh, to the north of Babylon on the River Tigris, had already been uncovered for half a century, and archaeologists were starting to appreciate the complexities of ancient Mesopotamian history.

Nebuchadnezzar's city extended over an impressive 7 sq km (3 sq miles). It was bounded by an outer three-part wall that, strengthened by towers and defended by a moat, was 18 km (11 miles) long and 30 m (98 ft) across – quite wide enough, as Herodotus explains, to allow a horse-drawn chariot to turn around in comfort. Within the outer walls, two areas were separated from the wider city. To the northeast lay Nebuchadnezzar's summer palace, known today as Tell Babil. To the west lay the inner city, the main ceremonial and political complex which spanned the Euphrates and covered an area of 5 sq km (2 sq miles). The German excavators, faced with vast amounts of mud brick, focused their attention on the east bank of this inner city. Consequently we know more about this part of Babylon than any other.

The inner city

The magnificent Ishtar Gate, named after the goddess of war and love, provided an imposing entrance to the inner city. This monumental gateway, built by Nebuchadnezzar, stood on a platform, had twin square towers and a 25-m (82-ft) arch, and was decorated with white and yellow dragons and bulls created from moulded bricks laid into the bright blue walls.

The Processional Way led southwards from the Ishtar Gate into the inner city. The king's palace was situated just inside the gate, between the Processional Way and the River Euphrates. The palace, like the gate, was built on a platform. It included five open courtyards, each surrounded by a multitude of halls and rooms on different levels, plus some partially underground vaulted chambers – the putative Hanging Gardens. The throne room was perhaps the most splendid room of all. More than 50 m (164 ft) long, it was decorated with glazed, moulded bricks showing a parade of lions and the tree of life. In the late 20th century Iraqi dictator Saddam Hussein had part of the palace reconstructed with modern bricks stamped with his name; today his reconstruction is being removed. Unfortunately, the palace has suffered badly from its most recent use as a military depot.

Further along the Processional Way were the two monuments that served as the religious heart of the city. Esagila was the temple complex of the god Marduk, which also contained shrines dedicated to other deities. The classical writers marvelled that the temple complex was rumoured to hold more than 20 tons of gold, including the golden statue of the god himself.

Etemenanki, or "the house that is the foundation of heaven and earth", was the mud-brick ziggurat, the original Tower of Babel. Unfortunately, as the ziggurat itself was dismantled in antiquity and only its square base has survived)archaeologists are unsure of its exact appearance.

The final occupations

Babylon was occupied by the Persians under Cyrus the Great in 539 BC, and then again in 331 BC by the Macedonians under Alexander the Great. In 323 BC Alexander died under mysterious circumstances in Nebuchadnezzar's palace. His body was preserved in a vat of honey, and taken to Egypt for burial. Subsequently Babylon entered a steep decline. By 141 BC, when the Parthians occupied Mesopotamia, Babylon was an obscure and insignificant town. Occupation at the site continued until medieval times, then petered out.

HOME OF ARTEMIS AND JOHN
Ephesus, Turkey

Site of the Temple of Artemis and, later, home to St John the Evangelist, Ephesus thrived under the Greeks, Romans, and Byzantines – all of whom left their mark.

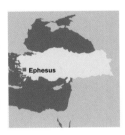

Ephesus, an ancient city on the west coast of Turkey, was famed throughout the classical world for the Great Temple of Artemis, one of the Seven Wonders of the Ancient World. The Bible (Acts 19:22) tells how St Paul, on a visit to Ephesus, sparked a riot as the silversmiths rose up to defend their goddess – and their business interests – crying, "Great is Diana [Artemis] of the Ephesians."

At the time of Paul's visit, Ephesus, which lies at the mouth of the River Kaystros, was a thriving port. Today the harbour has silted up, and there is no sea trade, but Ephesus now thrives as one of the most popular tourist destinations in the world, receiving an estimated two million visitors each year.

Early history

While Greek legend tells us that Amazons founded the city, archaeology reveals that the first traces of occupation date to the Neolithic period. Fortifications were built there in the Bronze Age. Next came a Mycenaean trading site and a Greek settlement.

The classical authors tell how the first city was built by Androklos, son of Kodros, King of Athens. Androklos had determined to build a new city in Anatolia, but could not decide where it should be. He consulted the oracle of Apollo, who explained that the site would be revealed by a fish and a boar. One day, travelling far from home, Androklos was cooking a fish on an open fire. But the fish jumped straight out of the frying pan,

and sparks from the fish set the nearby bushes on fire. As a startled boar ran out from a bush, Androklos knew that he had found his city site.

The prosperous port attracted a succession of rulers. There was a period of Lydian control when the wealthy King Croesus financed the rebuilding of the Temple of Artemis, the Artemision, surrounding it with housing. Next came a period of Persian rule.

In 334 BC the city was taken by Alexander the Great, and came under the control of his general, later king, Lysimachos. Lysimachos dredged the harbour, which had already started to silt up, reinforced the fortifications, and moved the city buildings away from the Artemision. Many of the surviving structures, including the theatre and the gymnasium, date from this time.

The Romans, and after

Eventually Ephesus was absorbed into the Roman Empire, becoming the capital of the province of Asia Minor. Again the city prospered, although an earthquake in 17 AD caused a great deal of damage that was repaired as the city was extended during the reign of Tiberius.

During the reign of the Emperor Decius, in the 3rd century AD, Christians were persecuted at Ephesus. Among the victims were seven young men who gave away their property then retreated to pray in a mountain cave, where they were walled in while they were sleeping. Almost 200 years passed before a farmer opened up the cave. The seven young men awoke thinking that they

Key Facts: Ephesus

Location: Western coast of Turkey	
Date: Multi-period classical and Christian site	
Discovered: Temple of Artemis discovered 1869	
Explored by: British excavations by John Turtle Wood in the	1860s; subsequent excavations by the Austrian Archaeological Institute
	Display: Archaeological remains are open to the public; many artefacts are in the Selçuk Museum. Finds from the Artemision are in the Istanbul Museum and British Museum.

had slept for just one night, and walked down into Ephesus, where there were amazed to find a Christian city. When the Seven Sleepers died, they were buried once again in their cave, which has become a site of Christian pilgrimage.

The city was attacked by the Goths at the end of the 3rd century, but recovered to gain renewed importance for pilgrims during the Christian era as the last home of both the Virgin Mary and St John the Evangelist.

Five centuries after John's death, the Byzantine Emperor Justinian (483–565) built a splendid basilica on top of his tomb in the Ayasoluk hills. Within the city proper, the 4th-century Church of the Virgin Mary was in 431 the setting for the Council of Ephesus, which confirmed the status of Mary as "Mother of God".

In the 15th century the city flourished once again under the Selçuk dynasty of the house of Aydin, which built an impressive mosque not far from the Temple of Artemis.

Excavation begins

The first official excavations at Ephesus were funded by the British Museum and conducted by John Turtle Wood, a British architect who, inspired by the biblical story of St Paul, had determined to discover the lost Temple of Artemis, the Artemision. After six years of patient excavation and several emergencies – he broke his collarbone in a riding accident, and was stabbed during the attempted assassination of the British Consul in Smyrna – on 1 January 1869 Wood discovered the marble floor of the temple at the bottom of a test pit 6 m (20 ft) deep. He uncovered the whole foundation before abandoning the site in 1874. Further excavations at the Artemision were conducted on behalf of the British Museum by D.G. Hogarth in 1904–5. Hogarth confirmed that the temple was in fact a series of temples, built one on top of another.

In 1895 an Austrian team led by Otto Benndorf and privately funded by Karl von Markhof took

Above: Although now a ruin, the theatre at Ephesus once housed an audience of thousands in one of the great cultural centres of the Hellenistic world.

Above: The architectural fragments that survive amply demonstrate that Ephesus was one of the great cities of the classical world.

over excavations at the city site. With breaks for the two world wars, the Austrian Archaeological Institute, supported by the Turkish authorities, has worked at Ephesus ever since, uncovering a series of public and private Greco-Roman buildings and investigating both the Basilica of St John and the tomb of the Seven Sleepers. Today the Austrians direct a multidisciplinary team that focuses not only on excavation, but also on the conservation and restoration of the finds. This includes the renovation of buildings, the re-erection of fallen columns, and the raising of a clear roof to cover and protect a substantial part of the ancient city.

The Temple of Artemis

Artemis, or Diana, of Ephesus was far removed from the shy, chaste hunter-goddess of classical mythology. At Ephesus, Artemis was a symbol of fertility, and she was adorned from her shoulders to her waist with what most archaeologists take to

be multiple breasts, although some have suggested that they may be eggs or even bulls' testicles.

While the classical historian Strabo tells us that the Artemision was destroyed and restored at least seven times, archaeology has been able to confirm four distinct building phases. The first temple was probably built around 800 BC. A subsequent temple was designed by the architect Chersiphron in about 600 BC. Chersiphron included tall columns in his design.

The Ionic temple financed by King Croesus of Lydia in about 560 BC was four times larger than the earlier building, making it one of the largest temples in the ancient world. Not only did his Atemision serve as a place of worship, but it was also an important market place, and an acknowledged place of sanctuary. Unfortunately, it was destroyed in 356 BC, when a young man named Herostratus made an ill-judged attempt to have his name remembered for ever by setting fire to the timber roof. According to legend, at the

Right: Diana, or Artemis, of Ephesus was a popular goddess throughout the Roman world. Here she stands, arms outstretched, her many breasts an obvious reminder of her fertility. The front of her robe is covered with the heads of many animals.

time of the fire the goddess herself was away, assisting at the birth of Alexander the Great.

The replacement classical temple was built entirely of marble and included many columns, 36 of which were carved in high relief, plus four bronze statues of Amazons. It was unfinished when Alexander the Great took control of Ephesus in 334 BC, and the conqueror offered to pay for the remaining work on condition that he be given full credit for his generosity. The Ephesians, reluctant to have Alexander's name carved on their temple, refused his offer on the tactful grounds that it was inappropriate for a god (Alexander) to dedicate offerings to a fellow god. They finished the temple themselves in 250 BC.

The classical temple was destroyed in a raid by the Goths in 262 AD. The Emperor Constantine, a Christian, was happy to restore the town, but left the temple as it stood. The surviving remains were burned for lime in 401, when a Christian church was built on the temple site.

ALEXANDER'S CITY
Alexandria, Egypt

The city founded by Alexander the Great became one of the foremost centres of learning and religion in the classical world.

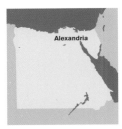

Alexandria is by no means a typical ancient Egyptian city. Founded in 331 BC by Alexander the Great, who was born in Macedonia, and later ruled by the Ptolemaic dynasty of Macedonian Greeks, it was essentially a Hellenistic city, populated by a mix of native Egyptians, Greeks, and Jews. Alexandria quickly became one of the most wealthy and sophisticated cities in the classical world, famous as a centre of learning and religious debate. It was in Alexandria that the Old Testament was first translated into Greek. The city survived a devastating series of earthquakes in the 4th century AD, and in 642 it was surrendered without a fight to Arab invaders who were threatening the survival of the Eastern Roman empire.

Alexander builds a capital

Alexander's new capital, 3000 years younger than Egypt's first capital, Memphis, was built on the site of an earlier, insignificant dynastic town named Rhakotis. The city occupied a stretch of land running between the Mediterranean Sea to the north and Lake Moeris to the south. This was an ideal location for a major seaport. The Heptastadion, a human-made causeway, ran from the city to nearby Pharos Island, creating an eastern or Great Harbour, and a smaller western harbour. Offshore, on Pharos, stood the great stone lighthouse that was one of the Seven Wonders of the Ancient World. Standing more than 100 m (330 ft) tall, the lighthouse tower was built around 280 BC. It was eventually destroyed by a series of earthquakes during the Middle Ages;

today the fort of Sultan Qaitbey, built in 1477, stands in its place.

Alexandria was built to a grid pattern. Two main thoroughfares, Canopus Street (running east to west) and Soma Street (running north to south), intersected at the heart of the city. Here stood the Soma, Alexander's tomb, which is now believed to lie under the Mosque of Nebi Daniel. The Palace Enclosure was an administrative centre to the east of the Great Harbour. The Serapeum, the temple of the god Serapis, lay in the south-western sector of the city. Nearby were the city cemeteries and the catacombs of Kom el-Shuqafa.

The Museion, situated in the south of the city, was the district dedicated to learning. Here stood the museum, and the great library which, housing an estimated one million books, attracted scholars from all over the Mediterranean world. The library burned to the ground in 47 BC, as Julius Caesar attempted to take Alexandria. Among the many important books that were lost in the blaze was the *History of Egypt*, a complete account of all Egypt's kings compiled by the priest Manetho for Ptolemy II. Luckily, fragments of Manetho's great work had been preserved in the writings of other authors.

A sunken city

As much of ancient Alexandria now lies under the waters of her harbours, the city has seen a series of underwater excavations. The first was conducted in 1961, when Kamal Abu el-Saadat discovered a colossal statue of the goddess Isis, an

---

Key Facts: Alexandria

Location: Mediterranean coast of Egypt

Date: Founded by Alexander the Great in 331 BC

Discovered: Occupied continuously since foundation

Explored by: Egyptologists and underwater experts

Display: Many of the sites are open to the public; artefacts displayed in the Alexandria Museum and the Bibliotheca Alexandrina

Egyptian deity who remained influential in the Greco-Roman world. More recently a French survey team lead by Jean-Yves Empereur, working close by the Qaitbey fort, has discovered a vast number of architectural elements, including statue parts, columns, obelisks, shipwrecks, and hundreds of masonry blocks which may be the remains of the Pharos lighthouse. Some of Empereur's finds pre-date the founding of Alexandria; it seems that Alexander and his successors imported antiquities from other, more ancient sites to decorate the new city.

A second French–Egyptian team, led by Franck Goodio, has concentrated on discovering the royal quarters of Alexandria. The team has so far announced the discovery of the lost Island of Antirrhodos, which, as the 1st-century Greek geographer Strabo tells us, was the site of Cleopatra's palace, and of the Titonium, the residence of Cleopatra's lover Mark Antony.

LAST STAND AT MASADA
Masada, Israel

The name Masada has become a byword for a free people's refusal to bow to tyranny, even in the face of overwhelming odds. But what's the truth behind the legend?

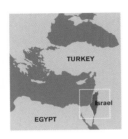

The rock site of Masada is one of the most significant locations in Jewish history. Here, the historian Josephus (*c.* 37–100 AD) tells us, entire families chose to commit suicide rather than endure capture by the Romans. Excavation, and the interpretation of the archaeological evidence uncovered, is playing an important role in determining the true history of Masada.

Herod's Palace

Herod the Great, king of Judaea, transformed the ancient city of Jerusalem with a mixture of traditional Jewish and Greco-Roman architecture, building a theatre and amphitheatre, and embellishing the Temple. Herod decided to build a new fortress-palace complex to provide both a comfortable residence for his family and a secure refuge in times of danger. He therefore selected a naturally defended location, a flat plateau on top of a rock 400 m (1300 ft) above the isolated edge of the Judaean Desert on the western shore of the Dead Sea. This site had already been used as a military outpost, but Herod improved its defensive capabilities with an intimidating series of walls and towers.

Herod's private palace, built between 37 and 31 BC, stood on three terraces linked by narrow stairways on the northernmost tip of the rock. A wall separated the palace from the fortress, guaranteeing the king's privacy while providing additional security. A second, larger palace stood on the precipitous western edge of the plateau. This was the administrative and political heart

of Masada, and probably included Herod's throne room. Water for the palaces came from enormous cisterns cut into the northwest side of the hill; these were fed by aqueducts designed to collect the winter rains. A smaller series of cisterns on the summit was available for use when the fortress was under siege. Extensive storage facilities ensured that the residents would not run out of food, while a well-stocked armoury ensured that there would always be weapons to hand.

The site was remote, but the archaeological remains of Herod's palaces suggest a luxurious lifestyle, with classical architecture, mosaic floors, frescoed walls, a balcony overlooking a breathtaking view and two bathhouses – a private one for the king's personal use and a multi-chambered bathhouse for guests. There were extensive administrative quarters and a synagogue, while more mundane items, excavated from a storage area, include food remains (nutshells, eggshells, olive pits, and date stones), basketry, textiles, wooden implements, and a wine jug stamped with Herod's name.

Rebellion

Following Herod's death in *c.* 4 BC the fortress became a Roman garrison. But in 66 AD the Jewish people started to rebel against Roman authority. A group of freedom fighters established themselves at Masada, where they made good use of Herod's buildings, and of the food and weapons remaining in his storerooms.

Key Facts: Masada

Location: Israel	of Archaeology, Hebrew University
Date: 1st century BC –1st century AD	**Display:** The site is open to the public. Finds from Masada are displayed in the Israel Museum, Jerusalem
Discovered: 1842	
Explored by: Yigael Yadin (1963–5); Ehud Netzer, Institute	

Roman siege

Four years later the Romans retaliated, attacking Jerusalem and looting and destroying the Temple. The Zealots – an extreme Jewish sect – fled the city, and they, too, took refuge at Masada. Almost impregnable, Masada remained a Zealot stronghold, housing almost 1000 men, women, and children until 73 AD, when the Tenth Legion under the command of Flavius Silva besieged the city. The Romans were unable to launch a direct assault on the fortress. Instead they erected an encircling wall, 3.2 km (2 miles) long. Eight siege camps were built, and finally an enormous, steep ramp of earth, stone, and timber was raised. A battering ram was then used to breach the fortifications. Today the Roman wall and camps are obvious at the base of the rock, while the ramp is still in place on the west side of the citadel.

It is not clear how long the siege lasted. Some authorities suggest two years. The archaeological evidence indicates that it may have gone on for several months, but some historians have suggested that it may have been over in a matter of weeks. With the rebellion quashed, and the rebels either dead or captured, the Romans again garrisoned Masada.

Finding the truth

The story of the siege of Masada inspired many explorers to seek out the lost fortress. The site was eventually discovered in 1842, but it was still more than a century before the first detailed excavations took place. Although the hot, dry desert climate had ensured good archaeological preservation, Masada, being remote and inhospitable, was a very difficult site to work. In 1963 Professor Yigael Yadin recruited a large multinational team of volunteers. Under his guidance, Masada

Right: The unique position of
the rock of Masada made it
especially suitable as a
formidable fortress and a
country retreat for King Herod
the Great. The lower picture
shows the remains of the
siege ramp built by the
Roman army when they
stormed the fortress.

developed a high public profile and quickly became a focus of national identity for the developing state of Israel. Today it is one of Israel's most important tourist sites, a place of pilgrimage that has come to symbolize the struggle of the Jewish people.

Alongside the large-scale architectural finds dating from Herod's time, Yadin discovered many smaller artefacts from the Zealot occupation. These included pottery, arrowheads, coins, textiles, and foods. Two Old Testament scrolls (fragments of the books of Deuteronomy and Ezekiel) were unearthed in a pit beneath the floor of the synagogue that, having been built by Herod and remodelled by the Zealots, is today one of the world's oldest surviving places of Jewish worship.

Eleven pottery fragments (*ostraka*) bearing personal names written in Hebrew were discovered in front of the northern palace. These pottery relics, one of which is inscribed with the name ben Yair, suggest a link to the story of mass suicide told by Josephus.

The evidence of Josephus

Josephus Flavius is the only contemporary writer to tell the story of Masada. Josephus was himself Jewish, and he played an active part in Jewish political affairs until he surrendered to Emperor Vespasian and became a Roman citizen. He was therefore well placed to tell the history of Masada – although, of course, his objectivity must always be open to question.

Josephus learned the story of Masada from two women who, along with five children, had hidden in a cistern to become the only survivors of the siege. He tells us how, soon after they had breached the fortress wall, the Romans retreated to their camp to enjoy a good night's sleep. This gave the Zealots time to develop a plan. It was obvious that Masada was about to be captured, and the Jewish leader, Eleazar ben Yair, gave a stirring speech. The Zealots would not face punishment by the Romans. They would commit suicide and face punishment by God.

The mass suicide was to be accomplished with a cold precision. First all the men were to kill their families. Then ten men, chosen by lot (the named pottery fragments?), were to kill the remaining men. Finally one man was to kill his companions and set fire to the site – only the storerooms were to survive this burning. The Zealots wanted the Romans to realize that they had chosen to die, rather than been starved to death. The sole survivor was then to commit suicide. In total 967 zealots – men, women, and children – are reported to have died at Masada.

Other archaeological evidence

Archaeologists have discovered evidence of extensive burning throughout the site, including the storerooms, but, as yet, the skeletal evidence does not prove the story of mass death. Three skeletons – a man, a woman, and a child – have been found in the ruined bathhouse attached to the northern palace. The female skeleton had elaborately braided hair, while the male (her husband?) was still wearing armour, which, archaeologists believe, may have been stolen from a Roman soldier.

A further 25 skeletons were found in a cave on the southern rock face. Initially it was assumed that these were suicides whose remains had been ignominiously dumped by the Romans. But the cave is difficult to access and, as it would have been far easier for the Romans simply to fling them off the plateau, it seems more likely that the bones are those of a group of Zealots who had been found hiding.

LOST WORLDS REDISCOVERED
Pompeii and Herculaneum, Italy

From their bars and brothels to their villas and houses, Pompeii and Herculaneum are perfectly preserved towns from the heyday of the Rome empire.

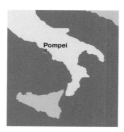

The remains of the Roman towns of Pompeii and Herculaneum in Campania, southern Italy, preserve a wealth of historic, cultural, and geological information thanks to a very specific and catastrophic event, the eruption of the volcanic Mount Vesuvius in 79 AD.

Evidence of the disaster includes a remarkable combination of written accounts, archaeological artefacts from body casts of the victims, the remains of the citizens' homes, gardens, civic buildings, and personal possessions, and the volcanic deposits which engulfed the sites.

Under the volcano

Among the victims of the eruption was Pliny the Elder, the polymath and statesman who wrote the multivolume *Historia Naturalis*. His nephew, Pliny the Younger, left a moving and detailed account of the event. The towns were destroyed by nearby Mount Vesuvius. The 1281-m (4227-ft) volcano was generally regarded as dormant, although in fact it had erupted as recently as 217 BC. By the 1st century AD the forests covering its slopes had been cleared for cultivation. Vines growing on the fertile volcanic soils produced some of the best wine in the Roman Empire, and Pompeii had grown into a bustling trade centre. Lying 8 km (5 miles) southeast of the volcano's summit, the town had some 25,000 people crammed into its narrow streets and crowded houses, which occupied more than 64 hectares (158 acres).

The nearby semicircular Bay of Naples created a wonderful natural harbour, and Herculaneum, one of its ports, lay just 6 km (3¾ miles) west of the volcano summit. The settlement is believed to have been considerably smaller than Pompeii, with an area of perhaps only 20 hectares (49 acres) and a population of around 5000, but as the town walls have yet to be discovered the full size is not accurately known.

Warning signs

The eruption of Mount Vesuvius was heralded by a catastrophic event of a different kind on 5 February 62 AD. The Roman historian Seneca reported that he had "just heard that Pompeii, the famous city in Campania, has been laid low by an earthquake". Herculaneum was also badly damaged by the tremors, which were felt as far away as Naples, and there is no doubt that the event was a precursor to the volcanic eruption 17 years later. Despite the widespread damage, the citizens seem to have taken the quake in their stride. They rapidly set about repairing and rebuilding their towns, which soon returned to prosperity.

In August 79 AD Pliny the Elder was in command of a Roman fleet at Misenum 32 km (20 miles) across the Bay of Naples from Vesuvius. As Pliny the Younger later recounted, on 24 August a mushroom-shaped cloud was spotted rising from the vicinity of Vesuvius:

> *It rose to a great height on a sort of trunk, and then split off into branches, I imagine because it was thrust upwards by the first*

Key Facts: Pompeii and Herculaneum

Location: Bay of Naples, southern Italy	**Display:** Both sites are open to the public; many artefacts are in the National Museum of Archaeology, Naples
Age: 79 AD	
Discovered: 1709	
Explored by: Guiseppe Fiorelli, 1860	

Below: **A grimly appropriate mosaic from the floor of a villa in Pompeii shows Death as a skeleton with a scythe and the inscription "Know thyself".**

Bottom: **Those citizens of Pompeii who were overcome and asphyxiated by the burning hot gas clouds from Vesuvius had no chance of survival. Archaeologists have made concrete casts of their bodies from the hollow moulds found in the ashes.**

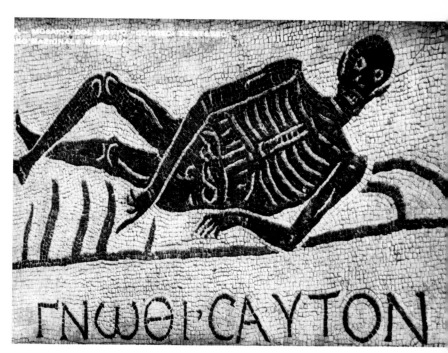

blast and then left unsupported as the pressure subsided, or else it was borne down by its own weight so that it spread out and gradually dispersed.

Pliny the Elder ordered the fleet to cross the bay to see what could be done to help. Hot ashes and blocks of pumice rained down on the boats, and by the time they reached the shore it was already covered with rocky debris. The sky darkened with dust. The 56-year-old Pliny landed at Stabiae to see the situation for himself, but was overcome by a fit of choking and probably poisoned by gases from the eruption. His body was found on the beach two days later.

Countdown to oblivion

It was not until 1979 that volcanologists were finally able to reconstruct the full extent of the eruption, which spread over the entire region of Campania. A major explosion at around noon on 24 August blasted some 4 cu km (1 cu mile) of ash and pumice 15 km (9 miles) into the stratosphere. The cloud later reached a height of 33 km (20 miles). This type of eruption is now known as Plinian in honour of its most famous victim. Within hours so much ash and pumice had fallen on Pompeii that house roofs collapsed under the weight and daylight was blotted out.

By midnight the ash was some 2 m (6½ ft) thick, and the eruption changed to a fountain of incandescent ash several kilometres high, with huge avalanches cascading down the volcano's flanks at high speed – a phenomenon known as a *nuée ardente*, or pyroclastic surge. Travelling at speeds of 100 km or more per hour (62 mph), these have huge destructive potential.

So far Herculaneum had been spared because the wind had carried ash and pumice southeast

over Pompeii. But during the night of 25 August the residents' false sense of security was demolished as a pyroclastic surge flowed through the town and into the sea. Reaching temperatures of up to 400°C (750°F), it incinerated every thing and being in its path. Repeated surges grew bigger and bigger until the fourth flowed as far as Pompeii and overwhelmed the town. The sixth surge reached even the outskirts of Strabiae, where its gases killed Pliny. Pompeii lay buried under 4 m (13 ft) of pumice, while the final deposit on Herculaneum was some 23 m (75 ft) thick.

Excavating the site

Excavations around Herculaneum and Pompeii date back to the 18th century. The theatre in Herculaneum was rediscovered in 1709, along with a number of bronze statues which were melted down to make medallions portraying the king and queen of Naples. Pompeii was discovered in 1748, but unfortunately the rulers

of Naples treated it as their personal treasure trove so that excavation was largely a matter of uncontrolled digging for any potentially valuable Roman antiquities, especially gold coins and jewellery. Even the British ambassador Sir William Hamilton, himself an avaricious antiquarian, complained about the destruction of "many curious monuments".

In the 1860s Guiseppe Fiorelli (1823–96) devised a more systematic excavation plan: he consolidated crumbling buildings and roofed them with frescoes and mosaics. He also discovered that, although the bodies of the victims had been incinerated by the intense heat, their shape and outline had been moulded by the surrounding volcanic deposits. By filling the cavities with a mixture of plaster and ash he found that he could replicate their shape. The famous images of a chained dog and huddled victims trying to protect themselves were obtained by this technique.

One private excavation by Gennaro Matrone in

1899–1902 found the skeleton of an old man wearing gold jewellery and surrounded by the remains of other wealthy individuals and their most valuable possessions. Matrone mistakenly thought the old man was Pliny, but this was clear evidence that many citizens had perished attempting to flee the eruption.

An everyday world

We now know that the town plan of Pompeii included an amphitheatre, a palaestra (an open exercise area surrounded by porches), and other civic buildings, as well as houses, taverns, shops, brothels, and more luxurious villas decorated with wall paintings and mosaics, and surrounded by extensive gardens.

The deeper burial of Herculaneum has helped to preserve some organic materials rather better than in Pompeii. Although carbonized, some wooden structures such as furniture and a child's cot have been found there. In a bakery, bread was found with the baker's stamp reading "Patuleius

Felix" still decipherable in the charred loaves. Perhaps the most important find at Herculaneum was the Villa of Papyri, with its huge library of some 1800 documents, many of which were still legible and provided invaluable insights into the life of the times.

The lack of body moulds in Herculaneum at first suggested that most of the citizens had escaped, but in 1982 hundreds of skeletons were found under beachfront deposits where they had tried to shelter. It is also possible that large numbers of victims are buried in the surrounding countryside, which is largely unexcavated.

The sites are now such popular tourist attractions that they are suffering considerable wear and tear, and looting is a major problem. It has been suggested that a replica of the site should be built for tourists, and that the original should be closed to conserve its treasures.

Above: **A view from the theatre complex across the huge site of Pompeii and the vastly bigger modern Naples might seem a safe distance from Vesuvius, but as history and present-day monitoring of the volcano shows the volcano is still active and potentially dangerous.**

GREAT ZIMBABWE
Masvingo, Zimbabwe

Europeans thought a "superior" race built Great Zimbabwe. The truth was far simpler: 18,000 people lived in a city built by Africans at the core of an African empire.

Great Zimbabwe, situated near the modern town of Masvingo, Zimbabwe, is an imposing complex of stone enclosures built by ancestors of the Shona people. Great Zimbabwe once stood at the heart of a vast empire extending into modern Botswana, South Africa, and Mozambique. Its kings controlled valuable trade networks that saw gold, ivory, and animal skins exchanged for cotton, glass beads, and ceramics. The empire's wealth and prestige were reflected in the size and sophistication of its city. However, the first explorers to visit Great Zimbabwe failed to understand its true significance. It was not until the early 20th century that Great Zimbabwe was finally recognized as a medieval city built by Africans, for Africans.

For gold and glory

In the 16th century, Portuguese soldiers based at the coastal fort of Sofala, Mozambique, had heard tales of wondrous ruins hidden deep in the heart of Africa. These, they reasoned, must be the remains of Ophir, the source of King Solomon's gold. The story of the lost mines inspired Carl Mauch, a German geologist who, in May 1871, set off in search of fortune and glory. He found Great Zimbabwe and, erroneously detecting the presence of cedar wood, decided that a Phoenician, most probably the Queen of Sheba, must have built it.

By the late 19th century Great Zimbabwe was no longer inaccessible. Tourists were visiting in increasing numbers, but they were blinded by their prejudices. Great Zimbabwe was clearly too sophisticated to have been built by Africans. It must have been built by a superior and more ancient race; if not the Phoenicians, perhaps the Egyptians, or possibly the Arabs. The same type of racial stereotyping was occurring at about the same time in Egypt, as some claimed that the pyramids were too advanced to have been built by Egyptians.

Overcoming prejudice

The British explorer J. Theodore Bent made an initial investigation of Great Zimbabwe in the late 19th century. Bent concluded that the site was not African in origin. In 1905 David Randall MacIver, working for the British Association for the Advancement of Science, made the first proper scientific survey. He discovered absolutely no evidence to support the theory of foreign builders. On the contrary, the artefacts were indistinguishable from goods known to have been made by local craftsmen, and there were just two imported objects, both dating to between the 14th and the 16th century AD.

Bent's conclusion that Great Zimbabwe was a medieval African city was so badly received that the British Association was forced to send another archaeologist. In 1929 Gertrude Caton-Thompson declared Great Zimbabwe to be "essentially African". Radiocarbon

Key Facts: Great Zimbabwe

Location: Zimbabwe, Africa

Date: Occupied from Early Iron Age until *c.* 1450

Discovered: Never lost to locals; officially "discovered" by Carl Mauch in 1871

Explored by: Initially explored by J. Theodore Bent (late 19th century), David Randall MacIver (1905), and Gertrude Caton-Thompson (1925). Subsequent investigations by a variety of western and African archaeologists

Display: The site is open to the public

dating of timbers subsequently confirmed her assessment.

Heart of an African empire

In 1958 excavations conducted by Roger Summers, Keith Robinson, and Anthony Whitty proved that, while Great Zimbabwe had been first occupied by an Early Iron Age farming community (c. 500–900), the impressive stone-walled enclosures had been built by Late Iron Age Shona (c. 1275–1450). At this time, an estimated 18,000 people lived on the site. With the loss of political power, and the inevitable depletion of the local environment caused by overcrowding, Great Zimbabwe was abandoned in about 1450.

The Shona of Great Zimbabwe lived in a well-stratified society divided between the ruling classes and the commoners, with social position reflected in place of residence. Their site covered an impressive 700 hectares (2.7 sq miles). On the top of low granite hill the king lived in the *dzimbabwe*, his court or house. Here, too, lived his immediate family and his advisers, and here were the ritual sites. The elite lived on the slope of the hill, while the many dozens of royal wives enjoyed a central location in the valley. Nearby stood the Great Enclosure, built from an estimated 900,000 stone blocks and housing a huge conical tower thought to represent a granary. The ordinary people lived in crowded housing in the valley.

Other *zimbabwes*, on a much smaller scale, have been found in the Zimbabwe culture area, a region that cuts across modern political boundaries to cover the old Shona empire.

Above: **At its height, Great Zimbabwe was home to an estimated population of 18,000. The surviving stone architecture confirms the skill of the ancient masons.**

HAVEN OF THE INCAS
Machu Picchu, Peru

In the 15th century, the Inca emperor built a religious retreat at Machu Picchu, in the Andes. Never found by the invading Spaniards, its remains evoke a vanished world.

For just over 100 years, starting in the mid 15th century AD, the Inca empire, "The Land of the Four Quarters", controlled a vast tract of the South American Andes. At its greatest extent, the Inca empire stretched from what is today southwestern Colombia as far south as central Chile, and included perhaps as many as 10 million people.

A spiritual place

In approximately 1460 the emperor Pachacuti Inca Yupanqui (1438–71) built a royal estate high in the mountains above the lower end of the Urubamba Valley, the "Sacred Valley" of the Incas. Pachacuti's site was well chosen. The Incas were a devout people who believed that mountain peaks and streams were the shrines or houses of their gods and spirits. Situated on the eastern slopes of the Andes between the dramatic twin peaks of Machu Picchu and Huayna Picchu, the remote site today known as Machu Picchu lay in the middle of a tropical mountain forest 70 km (43 miles) – a four-day walk – to the northwest of the Inca capital city Cuzco. Not only did Machu Picchu provide the emperor with a religious retreat, but it was also an ideal location for the royal astronomer-priests to record the movements of the sun, moon, and stars.

Following Pachacuti's death, the estate was maintained by his descendants, but within a few generations it started to deteriorate. By the time Spanish invaders reached Cuzco in 1532, it had been more or less abandoned. While the rest of the empire was overrun, the Spanish did not discover Machu Picchu and so the estate, never lost to those who still farmed on its terraces, remained hidden from the world until 1911.

Master stonemasons

The Inca architects contoured Machu Picchu to the steep local landscape, making use of natural stone formations wherever possible. The end result was unique: a royal retreat built into the mountain rock, offering a spectacular view over the Urubamba Valley. The estate included more than 200 buildings with a royal residence, more humble housing, sacred areas, baths, and tombs. But there were no administrative buildings, a clear indication that Pachacuti never intended to take up permanent residence.

Most of the buildings were made of large granite blocks shaped and fitted together with incredible precision without the use of mortar. These Inca structures have withstood the earth tremors that demolished many of the buildings raised by the Spanish at other Inca sites; some of their blocks are still so tight fitting that it is today impossible to slide a blade between them. The stone houses with steep thatched roofs and trapezoidal doors were either grouped around central courtyards or ranked along narrow terraces. Most were one storey high, although a few were taller, their upper floors being reached by means of a rope ladder. Water for the residents was supplied through stone pipes and stored in stone cisterns and pools.

Key Facts: Machu Picchu

Location: High Andes, Peru	**Explored by:** Hiram Bingham
Date: Built mid 15th century	**Display:** The site is open to the public
Discovered: Always known to local farmers; officially rediscovered by American explorer Hiram Bingham in 1911	

The most impressive buildings were the temples. The Temple of the Sun, a circular stone tower in the southern sector of the estate, was built around the sacred rock outcrop where the royal astronomers stood to record the movements of the sun. The Temple of Three Windows, in the western sector of the estate, incorporated a massive rock as the base of one wall.

To grow their crops, the residents of Machu Picchu constructed an extensive system of terraces watered by artificial irrigation outside the central estate. The terraces could have grown enough food to feed the inhabitants, but there would not have been enough left over for trade. Lack of storage facilities is further confirmation that Machu Picchu was never intended to be an agricultural or trading centre.

Quest for a lost city

In 1911 the American historian Hiram Bingham journeyed to South America intent on discovering the lost city of Vilcabamba, the last stronghold of the Inca people which, it was rumoured, was filled with their treasures. Instead, he discovered the forgotten site of Machu Picchu. Bingham always believed that Machu Picchu was Vilcabamba, but many archaeologists remained unconvinced, and the real Vilcabamba was eventually discovered by Gene Savoy at Espiritu Pampa in 1964.

Bingham had not always been interested in Inca sites. His first voyage to South America had been undertaken to complete his research into the life of the 19th-century soldier and statesman Simon Bolivar, liberator of Peru, Bolivia, Colombia, Ecuador, and Venezuela. But his brief stay in Peru

Above: **The Inca peoples believed that natural features such as streams and mountain peaks were homes to their deities. The terraced hilltop site of Machu Picchu was an ideal place to communicate with the gods.**

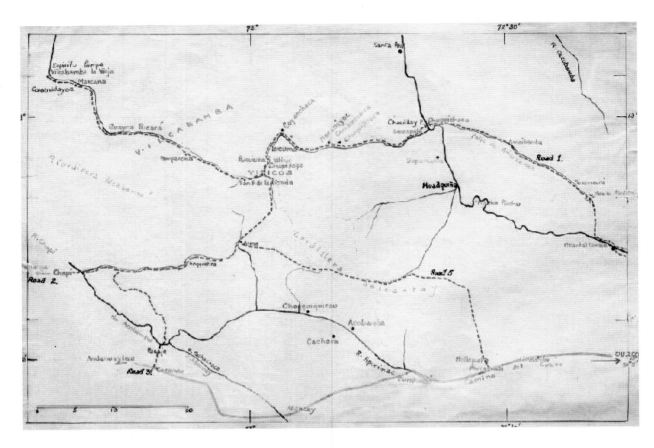

Above: **Original map of Machu Picchu drawn by the explorer and archaeologist Hiram Bingham, now housed in Yale University Library.**

was enough to spark his interest in discovering Vilcabamba and its treasures. In 1911 Bingham returned to Peru and travelled with a small team by donkey through the Urubamba Gorge, the site of many smaller-scale Inca building works. When a local farmer, Melchor Arteaga, told him about extensive ruins high on a mountain ridge, he set off to investigate. On 11 July 1911 an 11-year-old guide led him to a site so overgrown that it was difficult to make out the distinctive Inca stonework beneath. Only in the patches where the local farmers had burned the vegetation was the true potential of the site apparent.

Bingham made a few notes, sketched a few structures, then resumed his quest for Vilcabamba. However, he did not forget Machu Picchu. Several weeks later he sent a survey team to make a preliminary examination of the site, and the next year he conducted a more thorough investigation. His team cleared the rampant vegetation, re-housed the local farmers who were occupying the ancient structures, conducted a limited amount of excavation, then mapped and photographed the site. His atmospheric

photographs were subsequently published in *National Geographic Magazine* (April 1913), generating unprecedented public interest in the Incas. Today Machu Picchu, one of the finest surviving examples of Inca architecture, is Peru's most popular tourist attraction.

A royal observatory

The Inca peoples left no written records, and so Bingham had no idea what kind of site he was investigating. Fortunately, there were some written records available. The Spanish colonizers had never visited Machu Picchu, but they did visit other Inca sites, and they made detailed observations of these places that they would eventually destroy. It is by reading these Spanish records, known as "chronicles", that archaeologists have been able to understand the intricate nature of Inca society and the significance of Machu Picchu.

The chronicles suggested that the remote Machu Picchu, obviously not a city, had been built as a retreat by emperor Pachacuti. This explains why no rich burials have been found

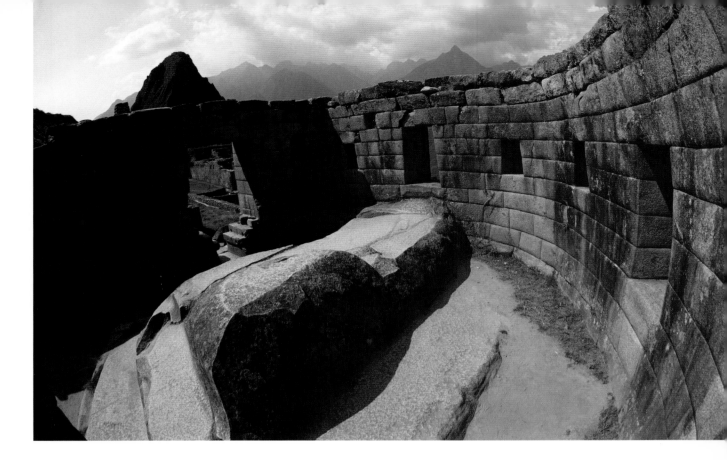

at Machu Picchu. Archaeologists have estimated
that although over 1000 people could have been
housed in or around the estate, the permanent
population is likely to have been far smaller, with
numbers swelling during imperial visits. It seems
that the Inca elite lived and died elsewhere,
visiting Machu Picchu for only a few weeks each
year. Only a small number of ordinary people –
caretakers and farmers – lived, died, and were
buried at Machu Picchu.

The chronicles also provided an explanation
for the freestanding carved stones which
Bingham found at Machu Picchu. These stones,
known as calendar, or sun, stones, were the
observation post used by the Inca astronomers,
who used their recordings to maintain the Inca
calendar. Other Inca sites had been equipped
with sun stones, but these were all too often
destroyed by the Spanish.

Above: The temple of the
sun was the focus of the
enormously important solar
rituals performed by the
astronomer priests of Machu
Picchu.

4

ART, INTELLECT, & RELIGION

Since the very beginnings of archaeology, one of the greatest challenges has been that of obtaining insights into the mind of our ancestors. Art of different kinds has been able to provide some great insights, as has the wide array of religious monuments produced in the past. Naturally, it is hard to make accurate deductions from such evidence in prehistory, but in periods for which we have writing a tremendous amount can be learned from the texts that have survived. Many of mankind's greatest achievements in the fields of art and religion are known to us only through the discoveries of archaeologists.

The study of past ways of thought, as deduced from material remains, is today known as "cognitive archaeology". It is by no means an easy task to assess the intellect of our ancestors in their absence, using only what they have left behind in the form of art and structures. How, for example, can we be sure that something is religious? It is a traditional joke that archaeologists always label something "ritual" when they can think of no other explanation for it. But the examples in this section of the book show a number of instances where, for various reasons, we can be sure that religion was involved.

In the remotest period, the Upper Palaeolithic, we have hundreds of decorated caves (such as Cosquer) and rock-shelters, and it is the art's location – rather than the content, which we cannot "read" – that can provide insights into the motivation lying behind some of it. Some cave art is on open view and was meant for the artist's fellows to see. But the fact that some of the cave art was carefully placed in remote locations that are very difficult to reach shows that it was obviously not meant for other people to see. Presumably it was offered to something non-human, whether god, spirit, or ancestor, and the often dire physical difficulties involved in reaching these locations certainly point to a very strong motivation which can only be described as religious in some way.

On the other hand, much of the world's prehistoric rock art, such as that of the Tassili N'Ajjer in North Africa, remains largely undated and, in the absence of any ethnographic information from descendants in the region, cannot be "read" in any reliable way. We can attempt to identify the animals depicted and interpret scenes involving people and/or animal figures, but the specific meanings elude us. It can certainly be speculated that rock art had many functions, whether of story-telling or conveying myths and social regulations, issuing warnings, and so forth, and some of these functions were very probably religious.

Similarly, the geoglyphs of Nazca, Peru, involved such effort in their production, and such careful planning in their layout, that they are clearly not simple random figures, and must have had tremendous significance to their makers and users, and quite possibly some links to astronomical observation. In the same way, great prehistoric monuments such as Stonehenge and Avebury have no obvious practical function, although they may have served as regional meeting places and so forth, and it is their occasional astronomical alignments which really help to pinpoint their probable religious role.

Actual testimony from descendants, even in the absence of written evidence, can also be vital to the archaeologist. On Easter Island, for example, whose script has not yet been deciphered, we know from testimony gathered by Captain James Cook and others in the 18th century shortly after the culture's discovery by the outside world, that the mysterious stone statues represented deceased chiefs and ancestors who were venerated, albeit not actually worshipped, by the islanders, and who were thought to watch over them.

Once an ancient script has been deciphered – as was most famously the case with Egyptian hieroglyphics thanks to the Rosetta Stone – then one can directly read texts and prove that certain buildings had a religious purpose, and even understand a great deal of the complexities of the religion and mythology in question. This is the key to our knowledge – for example, how much of the iconography on Greek vases could we possibly comprehend if we could not read Greek?

Where more recent cultures are concerned, phenomena such as China's Terracotta Army, the Dead Sea Scrolls, and the enormous religious complex of Angkor can readily be understood because we can read the scripts of these periods and regions – so we know a huge amount about the deeds of the first emperor of China, the beliefs of the Holy Land, and the mixed influences that affected medieval Cambodia.

GREAT STONE CIRCLES
Stonehenge and Avebury, England

Thousands of years after they were built, the stone circles of Stonehenge and Avebury still have the power to inspire awe and provoke controversy.

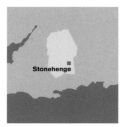

Stonehenge, Britain's most famous prehistoric monument, is a complex of stone and earth located on Salisbury Plain in southern England. Excavations and radiocarbon dating have revealed over the years that it is the remnants of at least three different circles

The first monument, dated to about 2950 BC, was a simple circular enclosure, an earthen bank with a ditch on the outside, and two entrances at the northeast and south. Such ritual structures, called "henges", are well known in Britain, although their ditch is usually on the inside. The depth of the Stonehenge ditch was about 2 m (6½ ft), and the chalk excavated from it was piled up to form the interior bank, which was about 2 m (6½ ft) high. Within this henge, a circle of 56 holes, now know as Aubrey holes (after their 17th-century discoverer, John Aubrey), were dug, but they do not seem to have contained posts or upright stones, and were later filled in – many contained cremation ashes. Also at this time, two great stones were erected at the entrance, one of which, the "heelstone", still survives.

Backbreaking toil

About 2600 BC the so-called bluestones were erected in a circle, after probably being transported about 200 miles (322 km) from the Preseli Hills of South Wales. Some specialists insist that the bluestones arrived in the vicinity of Stonehenge through natural glacial action during the Ice Age, but there is a total absence of such rocks in Wessex except in prehistoric monuments. So, unless we believe that prehistoric people used up every single large bluestone in the area, we have to accept that the rocks were brought in through human transport despite the distances and efforts required.

Finally, around 2300 BC, the famous trilithons – the great uprights of sarsen stone, a hard sandstone – weighing 25 to 45 tons, were hauled by hundreds of people more than 32 km (20 miles) to the site and set up as a ring of uprights with their unique lintels, together with an inner horseshoe setting of five trilithons (each comprising two uprights with a horizontal stone on top). The lintels, weighing 9 tons, were held in place through mortise and tenon joints. Excavations at Stonehenge have recovered an abundance of sarsen "mauls", battered round stones from tennis ball to soccer ball in size, which were clearly used to bash and shape the surface of the sarsens and bluestones, and to carve the mortises and tenons. A horseshoe of bluestones was set up inside the inner sarsens. The monument, approached by an "avenue" of twin banks 12 m (39½ ft) apart and 2.5 km (1½ miles) long, was abandoned in about 1600 BC, after 1400 years of continuous use.

The finished monument would have been visible from kilometres around, and many of the clusters of Bronze Age round barrows (burial mounds) were placed on ridges so as to be visible from the ceremonial site.

Pondering a purpose

Nobody knows who built these monuments or why. In the 12th century, the Welsh writer and

Key Facts: Avebury/Stonehenge

Location: Wiltshire, southern England

Date: Neolithic, *c.* 3000–1600 BC

Discovered: Always known

Explored by: Various British excavators – for example,

Richard Atkinson at Stonehenge, 1952–58, and Alexander Keiller at Avebury 1934–9

Display: The sites are open to the public; finds can be seen at Devizes Museum, Wiltshire and the British Museum

chronicler Geoffrey of Monmouth claimed that the magician Merlin had removed the stones from Ireland and rebuilt them in England; the architect Inigo Jones saw it as a Roman temple, while William Stukeley in the 18th century attributed it to the druids – as do many people today. But druids certainly had nothing to do with it, as they emerged in Britain more than 1000 years after it was finished.

Most likely it was a ritual site or a meeting place for ceremonialism, and it certainly had some astronomical or calendar function, as the sun rises over the heelstone on midsummer's day, and the monument's northeast–southwest axial alignment is also on the midwinter sunset. However, in the 1960s and 70s, the astronomical aspect was taken to ridiculous lengths by researchers who suggested that the monument had been an sophisticated eclipse predictor.

In 1953, some petroglyphs (carvings on rock) of prehistoric daggers and axe heads were discovered on one of the sarsen uprights in the horseshoe. Other carvings, much more weathered, were detected very recently by scientists using laser scanning technology.

Avebury

Avebury, 32 km (20 miles) away from Stonehenge, is in some respects a more modest monument, since it lacks architectural splendour; however, in other ways it is by far the more impressive accomplishment. Aubrey himself claimed that Avebury was "as much surpassing Stonehenge as a cathedral doth a parish church".

The largest stone circle in Europe, enclosing an area of 11.5 hectares (28 acres), it comprised numerous 20-ton sarsen stones, which were erected about 5000 years ago in a circle within a massive circular ditch and bank earthwork. The monument was under construction and in use for about 1500 years. Like Stonehenge, it was surrounded by a monumental landscape of tombs, enclosures, and ceremonial sites, including the famous megalithic tombs known as the Kennet long barrows, and Silbury Hill, the greatest prehistoric mound in Europe.

The original henge, far larger than that of Stonehenge, had a huge ditch that was 7–10 m (33 ft) in depth, with a width at the top of more than 23 m (75½ ft), and about 4 m (13 ft) at the bottom. The excavated chalk was used to build the

Above: An aerial view of Stonehenge showing the remains of the circle and inner horseshoe made of great sarsen trilithons, as well as some of the smaller bluestone uprights.

bank outside the ditch – it is about 1.3 km (1 mile) long, and would originally have been about 17 m (55 ft) high and about 25 m (82 ft) wide; it must have been a striking sight when the white chalk was still visible.

Circles and circles

The three great stone circles at Avebury comprise an outer ring of 98 huge stones just inside the ditch, with the two biggest standing at the north and south entrances to the henge; the two smaller inner circles are aligned roughly north–south. The northern circle, with a radius of 49 m (161 ft) and at least 27 stones (now mostly missing), has the "cove" at its centre, originally a three-sided arrangement of enormous stones. Inside the southern circle, 51 m (167 ft) in diameter and composed of 29 standing stones, there was a single tall stone, the "Obelisk", more than 6 m (20 ft) high. The whole of Stonehenge could easily be fitted inside either of Avebury's inner circles.

Over the past centuries, numerous stones were removed for building purposes or other reasons, and on at least one occasion someone was killed by one that fell. (During excavations in 1938, the remains of a 14th century barber-surgeon were found underneath – he had coins with him, as well as scissors. He may have been searching for treasure with a probe. His skeleton, lost in the Blitz, was rediscovered in 1999.) Although standing about 5 m (16 ft) above ground, the stones can topple because they mostly extend no more than 1 m (3 ft) beneath the soil, although in 2003 one was found which may go down about 3 m (10 ft), and weigh up to 100 tons.

Making improvements

Avebury's present appearance is largely due to the Alexander Keiller, who bought the site in 1934 and undertook considerable excavation and restoration – he knocked down buildings, tore down three-quarters of the village, removed fences, dynamited trees, re-erected megaliths,

and set concrete markers where he believed stones were missing. He also unearthed stones that had been buried by farmers and superstitious Christians, and cast them upright in concrete. His excavations recovered countless stone tools and animal shoulder blades which were used as shovels to dig the vast earthwork.

The circles were first recorded by Aubrey in 1649, and mapped in 1720s by Stukeley who, as usual, attributed the monuments to the druids. The main circle was linked to the "West Kennet avenue", 15 m (50 ft) wide, and with 100 pairs of standing stones which stood 25 m (82 ft) apart, and led to the "Sanctuary", a round timber structure within a stone circle. The avenue's stones were less huge than those of the Avebury circles, and in each pair one was long and cylindrical while the other was broad and often

triangular – inevitably sexual symbolism comes to mind here, as also with the cove and obelisk. A second avenue, the Beckhampton, was originally of the same length, but even by Stukeley's time was reduced to 30 stones, some still in pairs, whereas today only two stones remain standing.

The number of people required to dig the vast Avebury ditch, build its huge bank, and transport the stones must have been enormous, and testifies to a tremendous engineering feat and a remarkable organization of labour. For example, the ditch, dug through solid chalk with antler picks and bone shovels, required the removal of 0.12 million cu m (3.9 million sq ft) of chalk and its piling up as a bank. It has been estimated that between 650,000 and 1.5 million man-hours must have been employed on the ditch and bank, and on the transportation and erection of stones.

Above: **An aerial view of Avebury looking east, showing the remains of the great ditch and bank, as well as the surviving or re-erected stones.**

DISASTER ON EASTER ISLAND
Easter Island, South Pacific Ocean

The people of Easter Island erected monumental statues and other structures, but in only a few centuries this society collapsed into poverty and war.

EASTER ISLAND

Easter Island, or Rapa Nui ("Big Rapa"), is one of the most remote pieces of permanently inhabited land in the world. Roughly triangular in shape, it is entirely volcanic in origin and covers only 171 sq km (66 sq miles) in the South Pacific. The island is so remote – 3747 km (2328 miles) from South America and 3622 km (2250 miles) from Pitcairn Island to the northwest – that it is extremely unlikely that it was ever colonized more than once by people arriving in canoes. Certainly the archaeological record indicates a single unbroken development of culture from the first settlers until the arrival of Europeans.

People arrive

Radiocarbon dating and linguistic evidence suggest that people first came here in the early centuries AD. By the 7th century they had well-developed stone structures. Contrary to theories put forward by several people, particularly the Norwegian Thor Heyerdahl, the island's colonists did not come from South America, but from eastern Polynesia, most likely via the island of Mangareva. This is confirmed not only by archaeology and language, but also by anthropology, blood groups, and genetics.

Once they had reached the island, the settlers were cut off for centuries. Their first known contact with the rest of humanity came on Easter Sunday (5 April) 1722, when the Dutch navigator Jacob Roggeveen encountered the island and gave it its famous name. Subsequent 18th-century visitors included the explorers Captain James Cook and the Comte de La Pérouse. Every written account of Easter Island marvels at the huge statues and wonders how such an apparently primitive people could have built them.

Secrets revealed

Investigation of the island began in the late 19th century, but really came into its own in 1955 when Heyerdahl led an expedition of professional archaeologists, who carried out the first stratigraphic excavations and obtained the first radiocarbon dates and pollen samples.

In the 1980s British palaeobotanist John Flenley studied pollen taken from the core of sediments at the bottom of the freshwater lakes in the island's volcanic craters. Analysis revealed that Easter Island was originally covered with rainforest dominated by a species of huge palm tree very similar to *Jubaea chilensis*, the Chilean wine palm. Thus the first Polynesian settlers – probably a few dozen men, women, and children in big double-hulled canoes – would have sighted a densely vegetated outcrop. But they soon transformed the environment, introducing domestic animals (chickens and rats) and making clearings in the forest to plant their food crops (bananas, sweet potatoes, and taro). The island's birds, unused to humans, were easy prey, while the newly arrived rats ate their eggs and their young.

During this initial phase, the islanders constructed small, simple *ahu* (stone platforms) of the type seen elsewhere in Polynesia, with relatively crude statues on or in front of them. In

Key Facts: Easter Island (Rapa Nui)

Location: Southern Pacific Ocean

Date: Early centuries AD onward

Discovered: By the Western world in 1722 AD

Explored by: Katherine Routledge 1914–15, and various excavators since, notably William Mulloy from the 1950s onward

Display: The island's major sites are open to the public; finds can be seen at museums on the island, at Viña del Mar (Chile) and Santiago de Chile, and at major museums worldwide

the second, or "middle", phase of Easter Island's history, from around 1000 to 1500 AD, the settlers built many larger ceremonial platforms comprising cores of rubble encased with often well-cut stone slabs, and hundreds of large statues. The population increased, perhaps quite rapidly, and the corresponding growth in the demand for food led to the gradual destruction of the forest as land was cleared for agriculture. Meanwhile the continuing construction of statues required ever greater amounts of timber for rollers and levers to transport the rocks.

Above: **Some of the numerous finished statues standing on the outer slope of the quarry at Rano Raraku. Although often portrayed in cartoons and popular books as "heads", they are in fact complete statues, carved down to their abdomen, but have become buried in sediment over time.**

The statues

More than 800 *moai* (statues) were carved, nearly all of them from the soft, volcanic tuff of the Rano Raraku crater. The main tools were basalt hammerstones – thousands of them were left lying in the quarry. All the statues were variations on a single theme: a human figure with a prominent, angular nose and chin, and often elongated perforated ears containing discs. The bodies, which end at the abdomen, have arms held tightly to the sides and hands held in front, with long fingertips meeting a stylized loincloth. They are believed to represent ancestor figures.

More than 230 *moai* were transported from the quarry to platforms around the edge of the island, where they were erected with their backs to the sea, as if watching over the villages. It is possible that some were dragged horizontally into position, their path lubricated with mashed palm fronds and sweet potatoes. However, recent experiments have shown that another efficient mode of transportation was upright on a sledge and rollers, together with the use of levers.

At the most prestigious platforms, the statues were given a separate *pukao*, or topknot, of red scoria, raised and placed on the head, and eyes of white coral, which seem to have been ceremonially inserted to "activate" their *mana*, or spiritual power.

The statues on the platforms range from 2 m to 10 m (6 ft 7 in to 33 ft) in height, and weigh up to 83,000 kg (82 tons). The biggest platform was Tongariki, the 15 statues of which were re-erected in the 1990s. In and around the quarry at Rano Raraku there are still almost 400 unfinished statues. One of them, "El Gigante", is more than 20 m (66 ft) long, and when completed would have weighed up to 274,000 kg (270 tons).

Rise of the birdmen

The final phase of the island's prehistory saw the collapse of the earlier way of life. Statues ceased to be carved, cremation gave way to burial, and 1000 years of peace ended with the manufacture in huge quantities of *mataa*, spearheads and daggers of obsidian, a sharp, black volcanic glass. The conflict which led to the toppling of the statues ended when the old religious and social system based on ancestor worship gave way to government by a warrior elite. Thereafter an annual chief, or "birdman", was chosen each year at the ceremonial village of Orongo, where drystone corbelled houses were perched high on the cliff that separates Rano Kau crater from the ocean. Each candidate had a young man to represent him. Every spring, competitors had to descend the 300 m (1000 ft) cliff to the shore, then swim 1 km (½ mile) on a bunch of reeds through shark-infested swells and strong currents to the outermost islet, Motu Nui. There they awaited – sometimes for weeks – the arrival of a migratory seabird, the sooty tern. The aim was to find its first egg. The winner would swim back with the egg securely held in a headband, and his master would become the new sacred birdman. Orongo's rich rock art is festooned with carvings of the birdmen, sometimes holding the egg which symbolized fertility. This was the system that was still developing when the Europeans arrived, and which ended with the arrival of Christian missionaries in the 1860s.

Ecological catastrophe

The causes of the island's decline and change are complex, but the major factor was human colonization. Pollen analysis has revealed here the most dramatic deforestation in the archaeological record. From at least 1200 years ago one can see a massive reduction in forest cover until, by the time Europeans arrived, there were no large trees left. The imported rats fed on the palm fruits and helped to prevent regeneration. Without the palm and other timber, statues could no longer be moved (hence the abandonment of work in the quarry); ocean-going canoes could no longer be built, thus cutting the population off from a

supply of deep-sea fish; and deforestation caused massive soil erosion which damaged crop-growing potential. Chickens became the most precious source of protein, and starvation gave rise to war, perhaps even to cannibalism.

By 1722, when European explorers arrived, the island's population had been reduced to about 2000, living in poverty amid the ruins of their former culture. The palm tree and several other species were now extinct, leaving Easter Island with only one small species of tree and two species of shrub. Subsequent slave raids and disease epidemics reduced the population to a rump of just over 100. Scholars have had to piece together a picture of the island as it once was from the testimony of descendants of these few survivors, from archaeological and palaeoenvironmental investigations, and from experimentation.

Above: **The great *ahu* of Tongariki, with its 15 statues, had been overthrown by the islanders, then further damaged by a tsunami in 1960. In the 1990s it was restored and its statues re-erected by a Japanese crane company. This series of *moai* shows clearly that, although similar, no two are identical in shape and size. Note the *pukao* (topknot) replaced on one of the *moai*.**

GLORIES OF ANGKOR WAT
Angkor, Cambodia

Angkor Wat is one of the world's greatest religious structures, but it is only part of a vast spiritual and worldly complex built by the rulers of the Khmer empire.

The immense complex of temples and other buildings that formed the city which is now named Angkor, in modern Cambodia, was one of the major wonders of ancient Asia. Rediscovered by a French missionary in 1850, it was studied quite intensively in later decades, and French colonialists eventually established major programmes to research the archaeology of Indochina. In the early 1970s, the Angkor region was captured by the Khmer Rouge, which formed a military dictatorship in Cambodia. This government was responsible for a period of neglect lasting two decades, during which numerous priceless sculptures were destroyed or illegally sold, and vegetation was allowed to encroach upon the historic site.

Cultural crossroads

In the early centuries AD, this part of Southeast Asia was a rich source of spices and metallic ores, and as a result it seems to have developed important political, religious, and commercial links with China and India. By the 6th century Chinese records give the name "Zhenla" to the region of the Middle Mekong River. Nobody is quite sure, but Zhenla appears to have denoted a series of regional chiefdoms, each with big defended settlements, and temple architecture that displayed strong Indian influence. Many other elements of Indian culture were also adopted, such as the recording of deeds in Sanskrit and in Indian scripts, while Indian legal and political institutions were also adapted, and the Hindu and Buddhist religions were espoused. Indian styles of religious art and architecture became widespread, while developing new forms and local characteristics.

During the 9th century AD, Zhenla seems to have been consolidated into a single, powerful Khmer empire by King Jayavarman II. By 900, King Yasovarman I had moved his capital to Angkor, and from here the empire was the dominant force in Southeast Asia until the early 15th century, when Angkor was pillaged by troops from Siam.

Holy city

Although the word "Angkor" comes from a Sanskrit term for "holy city", Angkor itself was not a city in the normal sense at all, but rather a huge, sprawling complex of temples, other monuments, reservoirs, and canals that developed in different stages over the centuries. It is not known to what extent ordinary people lived inside the complex.

The spatial layout of Angkor was based on Indian religious concepts. It was constructed around a central pyramid temple built on Phnom Bakheng, the only natural hill in the area. This temple was linked with Mount Meru, the central mountain in traditional Indian cosmology.

Successive Khmer kings founded temples in which, at first, the central object of worship was the *lingam* of the Hindu god Siva; the *lingam* is a stylized phallus which also represented royal authority. Over time, the emphasis of Angkor's iconography changed from the Hindu cult of Siva to Mahayana Buddhism, but throughout the

---

Key Facts: Angkor

Location: Cambodia

Date: 9th to 15th centuries AD

Discovered: By the Western world in the 16th century AD, and especially after 1850

Explored by: Numerous excavators and scholars, primarily French (the Ecole Français d'Extrême-Orient)

Display: The major temples and structures are open to the public; finds can be seen in Phnom Penh and many museums around the world – notably the Musée Guimet, Paris

Above: Part of the sandstone temple of Angkor Wat; note the beautiful carvings of *apsaras* (celestial maidens who dance, sing, and otherwise entertain the gods) in the left foreground. There are about 1700 of these on the galleries and towers at Angkor Wat, each different in detail and gesture, with elaborate head-dresses and hairstyles.

Above: **Detail of the great 49 m (161 ft) long bas-relief at Angkor Wat depicting the "Churning of the Sea of Milk", a Hindu creation myth: *asuras* (demons) are pulling on the body of the giant serpent Vasuki, which is coiled around Mount Mandara – this churns the ocean and releases the elixir of immortality.**

period the overwhelming priority of the Khmer rulers (who were thought to be immortal) was to glorify themselves by building great monuments.

Angkor Thom

The Khmer kingdom reached its greatest extent during the 12th century under King Jayavarman VII. He built the Angkor Thom complex, which probably remained the Khmer capital until the 17th century. This complex covers 900 hectares (3½ sq miles) and is enclosed by a wall 3 km (nearly 2 miles) square. In each side of the structure is a gateway, 23 m (75 ft) high, which features a tower carved with four faces pointing to the four cardinal points of the compass. All the gates are approached by impressive avenues decorated with carved gods and demons.

The Angkor Thom complex contains a few residential structures (most of the original dwellings were probably made of wood and thatch, and have not survived), but there are numerous temples from various centuries, and in particular the magnificent Bayon where the four entrance roads converge. One of the greatest of Angkor's buildings, the Bayon probably began as a Hindu monument, but was converted into a Buddhist sanctuary before completion, probably during the late 12th or early 13th century. The structure has 54 towers, each decorated with four beatifically carved smiling faces of an Avalokitesvara (a future Buddha), together with incredible bas-relief carvings of scenes from everyday Khmer life as well as events in history, including great naval battles. To the north of the

Bayon stands the great carved Elephant Terrace, 3 m (10 ft) high and 275 m (300 yd) long, as well as many smaller temples.

Angkor Wat

Another successful Khmer monarch was King Suryavarman II, who in the 12th century built the most famous temple complex of all, Angkor Wat. This great shrine blended Hindu cosmology and architecture with pre-existing Khmer beliefs. The enclosure symbolizes the Hindu cosmos, while the temple itself stood for the five peaks of Mount Meru, the home of the gods.

One of Angkor's great strategic and practical advantages was its location on the shore of Tonle Sap, the largest lake in Southeast Asia. In the wet season, water from the Mekong River flows back into the lake and more than trebles its surface area to 100,000 sq km (38,600 sq miles). The lake provided a plentiful supply of fish, as well as water for irrigation. An elaborate complex of reservoirs, canals, and moats was dominated by two huge reservoirs: the eastern one was 7 km by 1 km (2.7 sq miles) in area; the western one was even larger. Chinese visitors in the 13th century reported that the people of the Angkor region had three or four rice crops a year, so it seems likely that the inhabitants had more food than they needed.

It also seems likely that a decline in this agricultural surplus – cause unknown – was one of the principal factors in the downfall of Angkorian civilization; another was the military expansionism of the Siamese. A further possibility is an increase in the incidence of malaria because if warfare had led to the paddy fields being less well maintained, then the water could have become clear and calm, and made an ideal breeding ground for the most dangerous kind of mosquito, which transmits malaria.

After the sack of Angkor in 1431, most of the complex was abandoned, but Angkor Wat was taken over by Buddhist monks and became a major pilgrimage centre.

Aksum

The city of Aksum (or Axum) was the heart of an extensive sub-Saharan kingdom which flourished from the 1st to the 7th centuries AD, the influence of which extended across the Red Sea from Northern Ethiopia to the Yemen. The city owed its prosperity to international trade. Aksum was an inland city with access to ivory, gold, and agricultural products. Control of the Red Sea coast via the port of Adulis allowed her merchants to link the eastern Roman Empire with lands as far away as India. Aksum quickly became a wealthy and highly literate kingdom, minting its own coinage and raising monumental architecture including royal tombs, stone stelae, and more than a hundred huge carved obelisks that acted as grave markers in the elite cemeteries.

The emergence of the Persian Empire brought the collapse of the traditional trade networks, and Aksum quickly declined in importance. Many of the obelisks were eventually torn down and smashed; one, seized by Benito Mussolini, was transported to Rome, but negotiations are currently under way to return it to Ethiopia.

Ezana (or Aezianas), ruler of Aksum (c. 320–50 AD), was converted to Christianity by a Syrio-Christian prisoner. Originally the religion of the elite, Christianity slowly spread through the population. There is an enduring legend that the Ark of the Covenant, the chest housing the Ten Commandments which the Bible tells us were handed to Moses by God, was brought to Aksum by Menelik, son of King Solomon and the Queen of Sheba. The chest was put into the care of the Coptic (Christian) monks, who have guarded it zealously ever since. This is, however, just one of many legends concerning the Ark of the Covenant.

AN ICE AGE ART GALLERY
Cosquer Cave, France

Of the many caves and rock shelters in Europe decorated by Ice Age artists, Cosquer Cave stands out as one of the most extraordinary.

The phenomenon of Ice Age art – works carried out between *c.* 32,000 and 12,000 years ago – is well known in Europe, especially in France and Spain, and more than 300 caves and rock shelters are now known which contain images from this period on walls and ceilings. Among the most extraordinary of these is the Grotte Cosquer, near Marseilles, southern France, which was first revealed to the world only in 1991. That it had remained concealed for so long was due to the fact that, while its entrance was originally 120 m (393 ft) above sea level, and about 10 km (6 miles) from the coast, a major rise in sea level after the end of the Ice Age flooded the shore, so that the cave's entrance now lies 37 m (121 ft) below the surface of the water. Moreover, to enter the cave entails going through a tunnel, 147 m (482 ft) long and only 90 cm (3 ft) in diameter, which is extremely dangerous.

Figures in the dark

The cave was discovered in 1985 by Henri Cosquer, a diver, who gradually pushed farther into the tunnel, then encountered the great cave at the end. The art, which he did not spot on his first visit, comprises well-preserved drawings in black pigment, negative stencils of hands in red and black, various engravings, and finger markings on the walls. To date a total of 481 figures have been found in the cave. Of these, 177 depict land animals – predominantly horses (63), ibex (28), and bison (24), as well as chamois, *megaloceros* (an extinct giant deer), saiga antelope, a feline, and other creatures. There are also depictions of marine fauna including seals, a group of large birds which may be auks, and some motifs that have been interpreted as jellyfish. In addition there are human motifs: a possible human figure, a phallus, vulvas, and the hand stencils. Another feature of the design is a series of complex geometric symbols (barbed signs, zigzags, etc). One engraving has been found on the cave floor, and in 2001 a semi-bas-relief of a horse facing left was discovered.

A large number of radiocarbon dates have been obtained from charcoal in fireplaces and some of the black drawings. These revealed at least two major phases of occupation – one around 27,000 years ago (when the hand stencils seem to have been made) and another around 19,000 years ago (when the black animals seem to have been drawn). There is further evidence of human activity in a number of torch-wipes on the walls, a dozen flints, and the handprint of a child.

Ice Age cave art

Although archaeologists have identified a number of caves that were inhabited by early humans, on the whole Ice Age people did not live in such dark, wet, and often dangerous places. They more commonly inhabited the mouths of caves, rock-shelters, and tents or huts in the open air. Cosquer was probably not lived in: the fireplaces in the cave may simply have been for illumination. The artists also used stone lamps that burned animal fat with a plant wick, probably for the same purpose.

Key Facts: Cosquer Cave (Grotte Cosquer)

Location: Near Marseilles, on the French Mediterranean coast

Date: Upper Palaeolithic, 27,000 and 19,000 BC

Discovered by: French diver Henri Cosquer in 1985, its art in 1991

Explored by: Jean Courtin and other underwater archaeologists sporadically since 1991

Display: The site is not open to the public

Above: **Bison, 1.2 m (3 ft 11 ins) long, drawn three-quarter face, which is quite unusual in cave art, but with a frontal view of its horns. It is clearly a male, and its tail is raised. Like all the Cosquer animals, its legs have no extremities. Charcoal from this figure, the biggest in the cave, gave a C14 date of 18,530 BC.**

The simplest and easiest way for people to make marks on a cave wall is by running their fingers over the soft layer that covers it, and there is an abundance of such "finger flutings" (also known as macaroni) in Cosquer, some of them descending beneath the present water level. The Ice Age visitors also used stone tools to carve on the walls, and in many parts of the site their engravings are more numerous than paintings; no specialized tools were needed to make them, as any sharp flint would incise the limestone.

Where pigment is concerned, the artists essentially had two basic colours at their disposal – red (which was always haematite, iron oxide, or red ochre) and black (either manganese dioxide or charcoal). There were various ways of applying these materials to the wall: they could be spat from the mouth, or blown via a tube (these were the techniques used for most of the hand stencils); they could be applied directly from crayons or nodules, or powdered and mixed with water, then applied with a pad or some kind of brush, or even with the fingers.

Finding a meaning

The figures in all cave art can be divided into three categories: animals, humans (always far rarer than animals – and Cosquer is no exception here), and "signs", which seem non-figurative to our eyes, but which may in fact have conveyed a great deal of information. Like many caves, Cosquer contains examples of all three.

When Ice Age art was first discovered in the late 19th century, it was assumed that the works had no particular meaning, and that they were simple decoration. In the first half of the 20th century, this view was widely superseded by theories about "hunting magic" and "fertility magic", despite overwhelming evidence to the contrary. Even though many people today still believe cave art to be full of hunting scenes, animals which seem to be drawn with some kind of missile sticking out of them are extraordinarily rare. On the whole, the ancient artists were not depicting the animals that they were hunting. Something else was going on.

Rules of the game

In the second half of the 20th century, attention switched to a structuralist analysis of the art, seeing each cave almost as a single composition rather than a random accumulation of individual figures, and quantifying the images as well as paying particular attention to the parts of the caves in which they are located. Some basic rules were discovered – for example, that horses and bovids (bison and aurochs) dominate, and tend to be, in the main, central panels, whereas carnivores (dangerous species) and humans tend to be at the back of the caves or in side chambers.

Throughout the whole period of cave art, despite variations in style, the artists depicted the same limited range of animals – almost always adults in profile, and no scenery: until the very end of the period, there were no groundlines, no landscapes, and no vegetation. We can grasp something of the "syntax" – the rules – but we cannot read their meanings. That is certainly the case with Cosquer: the paintings appear to be more than art for art's sake, but their exact significance can only be imagined.

Yet it is clear that the art did contain meanings and messages, perhaps of many different kinds: myths and creation stories, social rules, warnings, snippets of information. In addition, while some of it was obviously meant to be seen by other people, in many cases it was hidden away in niches, chimneys, or tiny chambers which other humans could not reach easily. Images produced in such locations, which the artist had endured physical hardships to get to, must inevitably have had some kind of strong religious motivation.

Where Cosquer is concerned, its present difficult location beneath the sea should not be allowed to exaggerate its air of mystery, as the site was far more easily accessible in the Ice Age.

Similarly, cave art as whole need not necessarily all be mystical, and it was probably not even the characteristic art of the period; instead, caves are simply the places where the art has best survived, but production of art in deep caves may well have been a very rare occurrence. We now know that the artists decorated everything, from the darkest depths of some caves to cave entrances, rock shelters, and rocks along rivers and up mountainsides – and doubtless also their tents, garments, and their own bodies.

THE PAINTED DESERT
Tassili N'Ajjer, Sahara

A large area of the Sahara Desert is renowned for the abundance and richness of its ancient rock paintings and engravings.

The Tassili N'Ajjer is a plateau covering 350,000 sq km (135,000 sq miles) and forms part of the Sahara, extending from Algeria into western Libya. The area has been inhabited since remote times, but it was during the Neolithic period that the Tassili really flourished, a mild and humid time when it was a veritable "Green Sahara" with lakes and marshes and a wide range of animals, birds, and aquatic resources.

Mysteries of the "Round Heads"

The earliest phase of rock art was that of the "Round Heads", so named because its human figures are depicted with circular heads and usually no facial features or hair. They are thought by some scholars to be black people, although convincing evidence is lacking. Some believe that this art extends back into the Ice Age, but there is as yet no firm evidence for this either.

"Round Head" art includes masked humans, anthropomorphs, animals, and symbolic drawings and geometric motifs. French archaeologist Henri Lhote and his team gave many of the larger and more spectacular images nicknames, such as the huge "big horned gods", or the "Martians" (figures whose heads look like divers' helmets).

There remain many mysteries in the Round Head art – not only the date and precise meanings of the images, but also their role. Were they religious or mythical figures? Were they created in sacred places that were the scene of formal processions or pilgrimages? Is the art primarily religious or secular?

Showing everyday life

The next phase is known as the "Bovidian" because its figures give a major role to domestic cattle and their herders. As the earliest cattle domestication in the region dates to around 6000 years ago, the Round Head phase must have ended by that period. The herdsmen of the Neolithic spread across the Sahara, and like their predecessors they decorated rocks and shelters everywhere.

The content of the Bovidian paintings is very different from that of the Round Heads – instead of the apparently religious or supernatural, Bovidian artists focused more on realism, everyday activities, and exuberant and even humorous themes.

The most common images represent the family group in its day-to-day activities: what seem to be groups of people talking, the herds and herders, hunting scenes, sexual scenes. The dwelling is depicted as a round or oval enclosure, with furnishings inside such as beds, tables and benches, utensils and pots lined up on a shelf. Children play while women sit chatting. It is women who are most often depicted with the cattle herds, which they seem to have guarded and milked. The men stand, their bows resting on the ground, while dogs, too,, are shown guarding the herds.

Archers are often depicted, alone, standing, running, or in groups; sometimes there are confrontations between two groups of archers, of both sexes. Tribes are shown in the course of moving, with women and children and baggage on the backs of cattle; there are images of dancing, and of boats that took people on

Key Facts: Tassili N'Ajjer	
Location: Algeria and Western Libya	scholarship in 1933
Date: Occupied since the Lower Palaeolithic, but the prehistoric rock art remains essentially undated	**Explored by:** Numerous scholars, notably French specialist Henri Lhote
Discovered: The rock art was first found by Western	**Display:** Many of the decorated sites can be visited by the public

Right: An engraving of a gazelle, attributed to the "bubaline phase", and about 50 cm (20 in) long. The lines inside its body are enigmatic.

Right: Painted scene thought by some scholars to represent the ceremony of "Lotori", a grand festival celebrated by the Peuls (Fulani), during which cattle were ritually lustered by being plunged into the water of a river or pond. Unfortunately, there is not a single clear depiction of this ceremony in the whole of Saharan rock art, so this interpretation remains pure speculation.

fishing trips on the rivers and lakes which then existed in the Sahara. The images of the cattle are often outstanding, not only in their accuracy and beauty, but also in their observation of animal behaviour. At the same time, paintings were produced of the wild fauna of this environment, including giraffes, elephants, antelopes, and ostriches.

Engravings

The Tassili engravings, particularly those in the Wadi Djerat, are among the richest such assemblages in the Sahara. They are distributed on the sandstone rocks of both banks of the dried-out river over a distance of 30 km (19 miles). A study in the 1970s estimated a total of about 4000 figures here. There is a great deal of originality, featuring very large images – often 2–3 m (6–10 feet) in length, although one giraffe is 8 m (26 feet) tall. Wild animals sometimes dominate the engravings, but there are also humans. There are far fewer scenes than in the Bovidian phase; instead it is more like an album of wild animal images, with only a small number of hunting scenes. But there are numerous therianthropes – half-animal, half-human creatures – which often indulge in strange sexual activities, and we can only assume that this involves a high degree of symbolism, ritual, or mythology.

THE DEAD SEA SCROLLS
Khirbet Qumran, Israel

The Dead Sea scrolls, discovered by accident in the 1940s, offer remarkable insights into both Judaism and early Christianity.

In the early spring of 1947, a group of Bedouin shepherds conducted an intensive search of the caves honeycombing the cliffs to the north and west of the archaeological site of Khirbet Qumran, on the northwest shore of the Dead Sea, Israel. They were looking for a missing goat or, perhaps, as some versions of the story tell, illegally searching for antiquities, but instead they stumbled across a collection of pottery jars housing leather and parchment scrolls covered in ancient writings.

The shepherds sold some of the scrolls to a local antiquities dealer and slowly, via the black market, the writings came to the attention of the academic community. The Bedouin were understandably reluctant to disclose the location of so profitable a find site, and the original cave, today known as Qumran Cave 1, was not identified by archaeologists until 1949.

A religious library

A further ten neighbouring caves have since yielded scrolls and many scroll fragments, including an unusual copper scroll found in Cave 3; all had been well preserved in the dry desert climate. Cave 4 was the most prolific cave, with more than 15,000 scroll fragments. The scrolls have been dated by radiocarbon dating to between 150 BC and 135 AD.

The scrolls are of great interest to students of both Judaism and early Christianity. They represent a religious library of between 800 and 900 documents written in Hebrew and Aramaic, some of which are copies of the same works. Their contents may be divided into four broad categories: sectarian works (writings relating to a particular religious sect); apocrypha (works which are excluded from various versions of the Bible and included in others), including new stories about Enoch, Noah, and Abraham; more general and administrative writings including the "Manual of Discipline", a book of rules for a religious community; and biblical works including the earliest known versions of some of the books of the Bible. There are 19 copies of the Book of Isaiah, including the relatively intact Isaiah scroll, which is an impressive 7 m (22 ft) long.

Who wrote the scrolls?

Many experts believe that the Dead Sea scrolls represent the library of the Essene Jews, a strict Messianic sect led by a "Teacher of Righteousness", who may have occupied the nearby settlement of Qumran from the late 2nd century BC until the 1st century AD. The Essenes, who had much in common with the early Christians, are mentioned by the Jewish historian Josephus, but are not mentioned in the New Testament. The archaeological investigation of Qumran, conducted during the 1950s, revealed a fortified settlement, but failed to find any clear link between the settlement and the scrolls. Archaeologists at the time called one building at Qumran the "scriptorium", or writing room, but other experts have since queried this

Key Facts: Dead Sea Scrolls

Location: Israel

Date: Radiocarbon dated to between 150 BC and 135 AD

Discovered: 1947

Explored by: Studied by various scholars both in Israel and the wider academic community

Display: The Shrine of the Book Museum and the Rockefeller Museum, Jerusalem

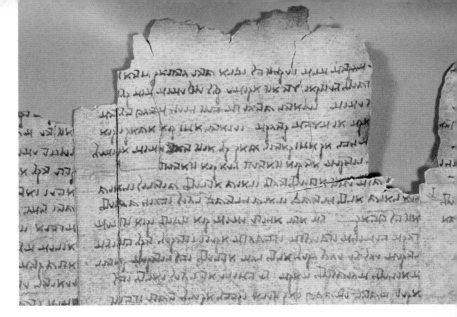

identification. They point out that the room's long "writing tables" are more likely to have been benches.

Other scholars, highlighting the discovery of similar scrolls at other Israeli sites, including Masada, have argued that the Dead Sea scrolls are perhaps the remains of the lost libraries of Jerusalem. Whatever their origins, it seems likely that the writings were hidden in the Qumran caves to protect them from the Romans during the First Jewish Revolt of 66 AD, which eventually led to the siege and sacking of Jerusalem and the looting and destruction of the Temple and its library in 70 AD.

Slow progress

The scrolls have had a controversial history since being discovered. The scrolls from Caves 1 and 2 were held by the Israeli authorities and published in the 1950s. These are today housed in the Shrine of the Book Museum, Jerusalem. The remaining scrolls and fragments, which are now housed in the Rockefeller Museum, East Jerusalem, were originally held by the Jordanian authorities, who gave them to a team of scholars to translate and publish. The same team continued their work after the Six Day War (1967), but progress was slow. Eventually, in 1991, photographs of the scrolls and fragments were released, allowing scholars worldwide to study the writings.

Top Right: **Part of the Scroll of Isaiah, one of the Dead Sea Scrolls found in Qumran Cave 1. This section is Chapter 6, Verse 7, and Chapter 7, Verse 15.**

Right: **The ruined settlement of Qumran, close by the caves which yielded the Dead Sea Scrolls. There is, however, no proven link between the settlement and the scrolls.**

READING THE ROSETTA STONE
Rosetta, Egypt

Hieroglyphs, the writing found on Egyptian monuments, held the key to Egypt's past. But they were indecipherable – until the Rosetta Stone gave up its secrets.

The ancient Egyptians carved their formal and religious texts on stone walls using elaborate hieroglyphic writing. Their more humdrum daily writings were recorded on papyrus in a more practical, simplified writing known as "hieratic". Eventually hieratic evolved into "demotic", an even simpler, and speedier, writing style.

The arrival of Christianity in the first centuries AD saw the closure of Egypt's pagan temples, and the scattering of its priesthoods. The Christians abandoned the old scripts and wrote using a combination of Greek letters and demotic signs, while their successors, the Muslim Arabs, wrote in Arabic script. Soon all knowledge of how to read Egypt's ancient writings was lost. Hand in hand with the loss of the texts went the loss of Egypt's written history.

Fifteen centuries later, Western historians had developed a keen interest in Egypt and its lost past. They were determined to decipher the hieroglyphic texts that decorated so many monuments. But without a key, their task seemed hopeless.

Finding the keystone

In July 1799, Napoleon's soldiers were engaged in reinforcing the defences at Fort Julien, the old medieval coastal fortress of Rosetta, which lay 80 km (50 miles) to the east of Alexandria. As they worked they came across a curious stone – a dark grey, damaged granite slab the polished face of which was inscribed in three different types of script. The stone was quickly taken to Cairo for further study.

One of the scripts was recognizable, and readable, as a Greek text written in Greek letters. It was a decree issued by the priesthood of Memphis on 27 March 196 BC in honour of the anniversary of the accession of the pharaoh Ptolemy V Epiphanes. The other two scripts were hieroglyphic and demotic. Most excitingly, the Greek text confirmed that the two unreadable texts were copies, in the Egyptian language, of the same decree. These three versions, in two languages, of the same decree offered scholars a real possibility of decoding the ancient writings and language.

Decipherment begins

Copies of the stone were made and sent to Paris, while the original was transported to London. In 1802 the Rosetta Stone was presented to the British Museum, where it remains today. Here, in a misguided effort to make the stone more readable, the incised figures were whitened, and the grey stone was darkened so that it took on the appearance of basalt. Today the Rosetta Stone has been restored to its original appearance, although a small, darkened square has been deliberately left untouched for comparison.

All over Europe scholars set to work, spending hours poring over their copies of the stone. In France the brilliant young linguist Jean-François Champollion (1790–1832) had dedicated his life to solving the mystery. By late 1821 he had made definite progress. He had realized that demotic

Key Facts: The Rosetta Stone

Location: Discovered at Fort Julien (Borg Rashid), near Rosetta, north west Nile Delta, Egypt

Date: The text on the stone was inscribed in 196 BC

Discovered: By Napoleon's troops in 1799

Explored by: The hieroglyphic text on the stone was eventually decoded by Jean-François Champollion

Display: The British Museum, London

16. On donnait ordinairement des chairs *jaunes* aux figures de *femmes*, et leurs vêtements variaient en *blanc*, en *vert* et en *rouge*.

Les mêmes règles sont suivies dans le coloriage des hiéroglyphes dessinés en petit sur les stèles, les sarcophages et cercueils ; mais les vêtements sont tous de couleur verte.

17. Dans tous les cas, si les signes hiéroglyphiques retracent les formes des différents *membres du corps* humain, ils sont toujours peints de *couleur rouge*,

ainsi que certains membres d'animaux, tels que la *tête de veau*, la

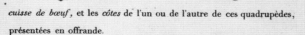

cuisse de bœuf, et les *côtes* de l'un ou de l'autre de ces quadrupèdes, présentées en offrande.

18. On appliquait aux caractères sculptés sur les monuments de premier ordre, des couleurs à peu près analogues à celles qui caractérisent l'être dont ils reproduisent l'image. C'est dans ce système que sont peints les grands hiéroglyphes représentant :

1° Des QUADRUPÈDES, tels que le *lion*, le *taureau*, le *bélier*, etc.

was a later, simplified version of hieratic, and that hieratic was itself a later, simplified form of hieroglyphics. This allowed him to devise a table comparing more than 300 hieroglyphic, hieratic, and demotic signs.

He knew that the Egyptians always wrote the names of their kings and queens inside cartouches, or ovals, and this knowledge allowed him to identify and read the names "Cleopatra" and "Ptolemy" on the Rosetta Stone. He also came to realize that hieroglyphics involved a mixture of alphabetic letters and non-alphabetic signs.

Champollion cracks the code

But the Rosetta Stone was broken; part of its hieroglyphic decree was missing. If further progress was to be made, Champollion needed to study a wider range of texts. On 14 September 1822, he started to examine copies of the inscriptions decorating the Great Temple built by Ramesses II at Abu Simbel, Nubia. These inscriptions were genuine dynastic Egyptian writings, 15 centuries older than the Greek text preserved on the Rosetta Stone. Automatically he picked out the cartouches that encircled the royal names and found, to his great astonishment, that he was able to read the names of Ramesses and Thothmes, or Tuthmosis. The code had finally started to crack.

Champollion continued his work, and in 1824 published his work *Précis du système hiéroglyphique des anciens Égyptians*, the world's first Egyptian grammar.

Above left: A page from Jean-François Champollion's *Egyptian Grammar* showing various hieroglyphic signs.

Above right: **The three scripts of the Rosetta Stone: top, hieroglyphs; middle, demotic; bottom, Greek. The stone has now been cleaned to reveal its original grey colour. Experts believe that the writing may originally have been coloured red.**

AN ARMY OF CLAY
Xi'an, China

Sparing no expense, a Chinese emperor manufactured and buried a fabulous terracotta army of soldiers, officers, and horses to guard his tomb.

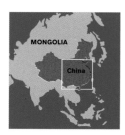

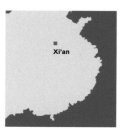

Often dubbed the Eighth Wonder of the World, the "terracotta army" was discovered in 1974 near the ancient capital of Xi'an, in China's Shaanxi province, by a group of peasants digging a well. At a depth of 3 m (10 ft) they found a 2200-year-old clay head of a general, and arms entangled in ancient bamboo matting. The fragments proved to be part of an underground army of about 8000 life-size figures in fired clay, distributed over an area of several square kilometres. The figures represent the troops who were to guard China's first emperor, Qin Shihuangdi, after his death in 210 BC.

Individual warriors

Large collections of small clay human figures are common in early Chinese aristocratic graves, but the life-size terracotta army is unique and spectacular. Each warrior's head is different and individual, fitted to a standardized body, and with a wide range of facial expressions, giving a sense of realism. Every racial group in China seems to be represented. More than half the warriors have been found to have round earlobes, but nearly 20 per cent have square ones, a proportion similar to modern Chinese. There are 25 styles of beard, corresponding to the age, character, facial shape, and post of the figure represented.

Much has also been learned from the figures about contemporary hairstyles, clothing, armour, weaponry, horse trappings, and the positioning of types of soldier. There are generals, officers, infantrymen, kneeling archers, and cavalrymen; more than 600 clay horses and more than 100 war chariots have also been uncovered. Most of the warriors are muscular, arranged in ancient Chinese battle formation.

Making and burying an army

The full names of 85 different sculptors have been found discreetly engraved and sealed under the armpits or beneath the long coats of the warriors. These craftsmen used local clay, fired at a very high temperature (around 800°C/ 1470°F), which gave the pottery a greyish surface colour. The figures were then painted with different colours to reproduce the details of soldiers' uniforms. The fact that the figures remain as hard as rock despite being buried for more than two millennia testifies to the skill of the ancient potters in achieving an accurate firing temperature.

Archaeologists estimate that the complex of pits has a floor space of 25,388 sq m (30,364 sq yd), and required the removal of 10,0000 cu m (130,800 cu yd) of earth. The pits were roofed with 8000 cu m (10,464 cu yd) of wood, mostly huge pines and cypresses. The floors were paved with 250,000 fired clay bricks.

Together with the terracotta army itself, this project must have cost enormous sums of money and involved an incredible amount of manpower. It is known that immediately he ascended the throne, the emperor ordered the construction of this huge mausoleum to begin and that a force

Key Facts: Terracotta Army

Location: Xi'an, Shaanxi province, China	**Display:** The main army is open to the public
Date: 3rd century BC	
Discovered: By peasants in 1974	
Explored by: Chinese archaeologists ever since	

of 700,000 slave labourers, architects, and artisans worked on the project for 36 years until the emperor's sudden death.

Inside the pits

The enormous Pit 1, which contains most of the figures, had been destroyed by fire; it is now enclosed within a hangar and forms one of China's – indeed the world's – major tourist attractions. More than 6000 soldiers stand in orderly rows, separated by walls of rammed earth. The roof of the pit, originally a crossbeam construction, seems to have burned down when rebels stole the metal weapons only 30 years after the emperor's death.

Pit 2, although smaller than Pit 1, contains a better range and quality of warriors. Now contained within a building for protection from the elements, it has a burnt and collapsed roof of pine and cypress logs, and was entered by five sloping ramps on the east and west. The pottery figures are laid out in an L-shape, surrounded by four smaller formations. There are thought to be about 1300 figures of men and horses in Pit 2, with 80 wooden chariots. In the 1990s, a newly excavated area of 9838 sq m (32,280 sq ft) yielded another 86 warriors and 44 horses, but these figures were rather different from those uncovered before – the warriors ride in horse-drawn chariots or kneel to shoot arrows and lead horses.

Chinese archaelogists found that Pit 3, discovered in 1976 had collapsed naturally, damaging the contents badly. This pit is about

Above: A view of a small part of the army still in situ in Pit 1. Note the walls of rammed earth separating the different groups of figures of soldiers and horses.

21 m (70 ft) long and 17.6 m (57 ft 9 in) wide, and more than 5 m (16 ft 5 in) deep. It contains 68 warriors, 4 horses, and a war chariot, as well as 34 weapons. This pit seems to represent the headquarters, the army's commanders, together with their personal guard – these warriors are at least 13 cm (5 in) taller than average soldiers, and they are drawn up in battle formation.

The emperor's tomb

The emperor himself lies undisturbed in a huge burial mound of rammed earth about 1.6 km (1 mile) to the west of his terracotta troops. The mound is 47 m (154 ft) tall, surrounded by two walls, and planted with pomegranate trees. According to contemporary accounts, the mound contains booby traps, as well as a three-dimensional map of China, with rivers of mercury. It must have been stocked with an incredible wealth of grave goods, but may well have been looted shortly after completion.

In 1995, archaeologists unearthed the remains of sacrificial temples inside the mound, where it is thought ritual food was offered four times a day. The temples cover an area of 15,240 sq m (50,000 sq ft).

Another terracotta army

The terracotta army has been so successful in drawing foreign tourists and their currency to Xi'an that a new airport was built 19 km (12 miles) from the city. While a motorway was being constructed to link it to Xi'an, a new find was made in 1990; just south of the tombs of the emperor Liu Qi (188–144 BC) and his wife, a site covering 96,000 sq m (115,000 sq yd), the size of 12 soccer pitches, was encountered. It contains another army of terracotta figures, associated with two tombs, housed in 24 vaults about 20 m (66 ft) apart and in 14 rows aligned north–south. The vaults are 4 to 10 m (13 to 33 ft) wide and 25 to 290 m (82 to 952 ft) long. They are therefore smaller than the Qin dynasty pits, but cover an area about five time as large, and their different sizes may correspond to those of the army units they contain.

All the human statues are of naked men with no arms. They are about 50 cm (20 in) high, and the whole body is painted an orange-red colour, with hair, eyebrows, beard, and eyes coloured black. Their clothes, probably of linen or silk, have disintegrated. Some researchers believe the now-vanished arms were held on with rods of precious metal which were subsequently stolen, while other suppose that they had moveable wooden arms that have rotted away.

The figures have graceful forms and delicate sculpted faces, each one different in age and facial expression, which may range from severe to smiling. In their remarkable realism they resemble the life-size figures which are about a century older, but the Qin figures are hollow on solid legs (which made them easier to transport), whereas the later army is completely solid. They are accompanied by weapons of copper and iron, arrowheads and spears swords, chisels and agricultural tools, carts, jewellery, and coins – all of them, like the men and horses, one-third life-size. Hundreds of figures have been uncovered so far, and as excavation continues; estimates of the total vary from 10,000 to a million.

Acknowledging the discoverers

In 2003 the farmers who discovered the original terracotta army announced their intention to sue the Beijing government for cheating them of the acclaim they deserve. And not only acclaim – the peasants followed the correct procedures in reporting their extraordinary find, but were given a tiny sum of money each, as well as free access to the museum, whereas a local museum director received a very large fee from the government. Local officials have rejected the men's demand to be recognized officially as the finders and instead the region's state-owned water company now claims the credit for the find.

ETCHINGS IN THE DESERT
Nazca Plain, Peru

The straight lines and swirling patterns carved in the desert by the Nazca people are awe-inspiring in their scale and virtuosity. But why were they made, and how?

The ancient Nazca culture, which extended over much of Peru's south coast, is known for its elaborate and intricate tapestries, as well as for brilliantly painted ceramics depicting elements of the natural and supernatural worlds. Its people tamed the desert environment in which they lived, developed irrigation systems to water their crops, and produced an abundance of food. They constructed platform mounds and mud-brick pyramids, and thousands of people were buried in their cemeteries. But for many people, this culture is best known for creating the Nazca lines.

A worldwide tradition

Geoglyphs, or ground drawings, are the most enormous images ever produced by prehistoric people. The most durable of them are the desert intaglios, made in rocky or desert areas by moving aside stones coated with a natural varnish to expose the lighter-coloured soil beneath. These exist in Australia, Arizona, and California; there are thousands in the Atacama Desert of northern Chile, but by far the most famous are the hundreds of spectacular and gigantic markings on the plain at Nazca.

Most clearly visible from the air (like most geoglyphs), these images – birds, a monkey, a spider, whales, etc., up to 200 m (650 ft) in length – are found among geometric figures such as triangles and trapezoids measuring up to 3 sq km (1 sq mile). In addition there are numerous straight lines up to 10 km (6 miles) in length, which some believe to be ceremonial pathways, although others see a great deal of astronomical or calendric significance in the Nazca layout, with the images perhaps representing particular constellations.

Dating and protecting the lines

After the dark, well-varnished cobbles were moved aside to make the figures, organic material accumulated on the lighter cobbles beneath and was encapsulated in new rock varnish. Radiocarbon dating of this organic matter has provided results from 190 BC to 660 AD This timeframe is confirmed by the distinct similarities between the animal figures and images on the pottery of the Nazca culture of 100–500 AD. However, pottery fragments in the area span a period from about 2000 BC to the Spanish colonial period, after 1532 AD, suggesting that line construction and use took place over a very long time.

The Nazca lines were doubtless always known to locals, but were first discovered by outsiders from the air in the 1920s. However, they have become most associated with the work of German mathematician Maria Reiche who, from the end of World War II, devoted her life to them, discovering the monkey with its spiral tail in 1946, and the spider. She not only brought them to the attention of scholars, but also made great efforts to preserve them and protect them from vandalism. They have become a major tourist attraction.

Key Facts: Nazca Plain

Location: Southern Peru

Date: 190 BC–660 AD

Discovered: By the world of scholarship in the 1920s

Explored by: Maria Reiche from the 1940s onwards, and many other specialists since

Display: The area can be visited easily

Sacred pathways?

Many of the straight lines radiate out from single points (line centres) which are often low hilltops or the ends of ridges – broken pottery found at these sites suggests that religious offerings were made there. Some investigators have suggested that the lines may point to sacred places such as mountains or that they were related to water and irrigation. Many of the lines seem to have served as pathways, probably for religious processions; most of the animal figures are formed by a single line, so that one can "enter", walk round the whole design, and "leave" without crossing or retracing one's steps.

Creating the patterns

Experiments show that the straight lines were very easy to produce, with the simplest of technologies. The great animal figures were probably drawn in miniature, then perhaps hugely expanded onto the landscape by means of a simple grid. The fact that some are best seen from above – rather than from neighbouring hills – does not mean that they ever were in the past (although some have speculated that the prehistoric Peruvians had the technology to make hot-air balloons). It is far more likely that the lines were meant to be walked, and/or to be seen by the gods. In the same way, the cruciform design of European medieval cathedrals is best appreciated from the sky, but their builders never saw them from that vantage point.

Above right: **The great spider figure, which, like all the zoomorphic figures at Nazca, can be traced by a single continuous line that never crosses itself and ends where it began. Note the damage caused by car tracks.**

Right: **The so-called "owl man" at Nazca is on the side of a hill, rather than on the flat surface of the plain like most of the figures. His raised arm makes him seem to be waving at the viewer. Not all scholars are convinced that this is an original, prehistoric figure rather than a more modern addition.**

5

WAR &
HUMAN CONFLICT

Historical and archaeological evidence show that
conflict has been part of the human condition for
thousands of years. There may even have been
conflict more than 30,000 years ago when modern
humans first encountered Neanderthal people.
The cause of such conflict is not too difficult to
imagine when you consider that groups of early
human hunters had to compete across the same
territory for the same game resources. From
weapon-damaged skeletons to the remains of
fortifications and sunken warships, the
archaeological record provides sober reminders of
our propensity to fight each other to the death.

Perhaps the earliest archaeological evidence of interpersonal conflict dates back more than 50,000 years. A Neanderthal skeleton from Shanidar in northern Iraq preserves a cut mark deep in a rib-bone. The wound can only have been inflicted by a sharp blade thrust by a right-handed assailant into the male victim's chest. Surprisingly, the victim survived the assault, as evidenced by a partial bony overgrowth of the wound. Our Cro-Magnon human ancestors may have accelerated the demise of the Neanderthals, but as yet there is no archaeological evidence to support this "genocide" theory. However, rock art from Australia, which is many thousands of years old, clearly shows evidence of warfare, with spear-carrying human figures using their weapons against each other rather than to hunt game.

The geographical separation of people promoted the divergence of language, which in turn led to increasingly important cultural and economic differences. From around 11,000 years ago there was increasing settlement of farming communities in the Middle East, Asia, and Africa. This led not only to trade between neighbours, but also to conflict. Environmental changes emphasized natural inequalities in the productivity of land and increased the number of boundary disputes.

The appearance of civilization in Mesopotamia around 5000 years ago brought social organization that subordinated the interests of the individual to those of the community as a whole. This development did nothing to reduce the incidence of warfare: on the contrary, it merely increased the human sense of the difference between "us" and "them".

By 5100 years ago several cities with populations of over 10,000 had grown in the Sumer region of southern Iraq. They were all independent states, and disputes between them were common. Technology was increasingly applied to the "arts" of strategy, attack, and defence.

All over the world, settlement and civilization were accompanied by conflict. Wheeled vehicles transformed both transport and warfare. By 4900 years ago the Assyrian kings of Mesopotamia were using light chariots for hunting and fighting. The domestication of the horse by farmers on the Eurasian steppes around 3200 years ago eventually gave armies increased mobility. Both the rate and scale of armed incursions increased by an order of magnitude that was surpassed only after the establishment of armed ships and navies.

Mycenaean trading ships plied the Mediterranean as long as 3400 years ago and it is likely that these vessels were also used for raiding overseas. By 3200 years ago the Mycenaean centres of power were themselves destroyed by ship-borne invaders from the Aegean about whose origins little is known. But they went to the Middle East and Egypt, where they became known as the Philistines, or Peleset. The Mycenaeans never recovered: their towns were abandoned, their people stopped writing, and their civilization was effectively lost. Time and time again conflict has produced "dark ages" such as this.

Gunpowder and firearms produced another escalation in the scale and efficiency of armed conflict which perhaps finally peaked in the mid 20th century with the development of atomic and thermonuclear weapons. Their devastating effects have been so horrific that a halt has been called to their proliferation.

From the archaeological point of view, conflict leaves many different kinds of traces and artefacts. These range from the remains of "hardware" or weaponry (from swords, arrow heads, and bullets to battleships), disturbed ground and constructions (trenches and forts), to evidence of wounds preserved on skeletons and historical data such as maps, letters, and photographs.

POSTCARDS FROM THE PAST
Vindolanda Fort, England

Tablets with messages written by ordinary men and women vividly portray everyday life in a remote outpost of the Roman empire.

One of the most remarkable recent finds relating to the Roman military colonization of northern Europe was the discovery of numerous wooden postcard-sized tablets which were thrown away just before the fortress of Vindolanda in Northumberland, northern England, was temporarily abandoned early in the 2nd century AD. The tablets are covered with messages written in ink by soldiers, slaves, merchants, women, and their scribes. They open a window on to the minutiae of life on the empire's northern frontier.

Soldiers from 22 different nations were present at one time or another: they came from all over Europe and as far away as North Africa. Their tablet communications provide an excellent source of information about the surprising diversity of people who occupied the garrison and had dealings with its soldiers more than 1900 years ago. Curiously, perhaps, they make no direct reference to political or military matters and do not mention any conflict with the people they were guarding against, the Scots.

On the frontier

The Vindolanda fort, high in the northern Pennine hills, was one of several frontier garrisons strung out across the border country between England and Scotland. The nearest neighbouring fort was at Corbridge, some 27 km (17 miles) or a day's march away. Vindolanda lies just south of Hadrian's Wall, a later construction begun in 122 AD to "divide the Romans from the barbarians". Vindolanda was first built in the latter part of the 1st century AD to support the Roman conquest of Britain. It was connected to the rest of the country by roads which facilitated rapid communication and deployment of troops. London could be reached in less than a week. There were some 50,000 troops stationed in northern England, largely Gauls and Germans recruited by the Romans as auxiliary forces.

Twentieth-century excavations of the site were interrupted by World War II and did not restart until the 1960s. The lack of any building work or significant disturbance, apart from the removal of stones for local buildings, since the Romans abandoned the region enabled archaeologists to uncover a wealth of information about the phases of the Vindolanda fort as the occupation force developed it from an initial wooden structure into more elaborate stone buildings.

The name Vindolanda may be derived from a Celtic word for "white" or "shining", and possibly referred to the appearance of the fort's external walls, which were plastered and whitewashed. All the buildings were timber-framed with wood-shingled roofs; the walls were wattle-and-daub panels, and some had glazed windows.

A chance discovery

A drainage ditch dug in 1972 to remove water from the excavations revealed a buried layer of ancient origin which contained organic material. Systematic exploration of this layer in the following year revealed the first of more than 1000 wooden writing tablets. Detailed

Key Facts: Vindolanda

Location: Northumberland, northern England

Population: From 72 AD

Discovered: By Robin Birley, 1972

Explored by: Team of archaeologists

Display: Online exhibition:
www.vindolanda.csad.ox.ac.uk/exhibition/history

examination of the deposit showed that there had been five periods between 85 and 130 AD during which successive timber buildings had been reconstructed one on top of another before finally being replaced by stone structures.

The tablets along with rubbish, such as discarded leather shoes and woollen garments, are surprisingly well preserved thanks to the dark, damp, anoxic (oxygen-free) conditions in which they were buried. Preserved leather shoes show that, despite Vindolanda's geographical isolation, its inhabitants were aware of and followed the latest Roman fashions in footwear. When first unearthed the tablets were in an extremely fragile condition – like soggy biscuits which if dried out just crumbled to dust. Like many ancient wooden artefacts they had to be very carefully excavated and conserved in a special environment.

The discovery inspired archaeologists to intensify their search for similar relics in other waterlogged Roman sites. They were rewarded with finds at Luguvalium (Carlisle), a fortification with a history similar to that of Vindolanda. The first building on this site was a wooden structure erected in around 72–3 AD; this was replaced by another timber construction around 103–5 AD, and finally by a stone fort in 165 AD.

News and views

The postcard-sized tablets consist of thin cuts of wood which were cheap to produce, durable, could readily take ink, and were reasonably light

Above: **Tablets from the Roman fort of Vindolanda in Northumberland. The discovery of more than 1000 of these thin, wooden tablets covered with Latin texts is one of the most wonderful of archaeological finds made in Britain in recent years. The tablets were effectively Roman "postcards" written over 1900 years ago.**

for transport over even long distances. The subject matter of most of the tablets is mundane, like that of most modern postcards which are open to scrutiny by anyone. Yet they present a unique insight into the everyday world and thoughts of the people who either occupied the Vindolanda camp or had dealings with members of the garrison. They have enabled historians to identify the main units garrisoned at Vindolanda and detachments from other units which were also stationed there from time to time. There are occasional references to London (Londinium), Gaul, and Rome, as well as to other places that have not yet been identified.

The tablets were used to exchange news and to send requests and thanks. There are greetings from former messmates, including complaints such as "I have sent you several messages – why have you not replied?" Another includes an all too familiar modern complaint – "*viae male sunt*" ("the roads are bad"). The requests and expressions of gratitude are mainly for everyday items such as shoes, socks, and underclothes, but there are also "thanks for giving us such a fine holiday", and "thanks for the oysters". There are orders for food and provisions such as "half a pound of pepper". Like modern correspondence, the letters begin with the name of the sender; this is followed by that of the recipient, then formal greetings, the message itself, and a formal ending.

Garrison life

The language ranges from finely crafted expressions of the elite which show a high degree of literacy to the more mundane colloquialisms of ordinary foot soldiers who may have employed scribes to write their letters. One tablet is an invitation to a birthday party to be held by the commanding officer on 11 September (the year is unspecified: that was normal practice) and indicates that there were women and children in the garrison. Another tablet is a child's writing exercise in which verses from the poet Virgil have

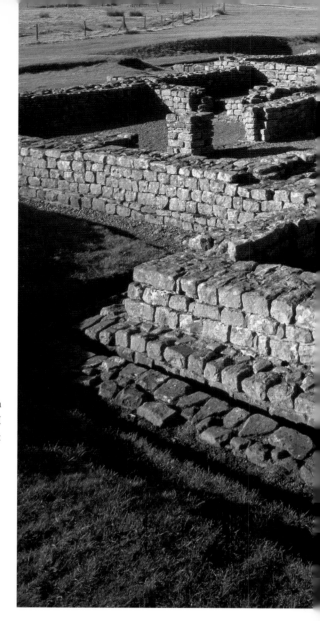

been copied out and another hand has added the comment that it is "sloppy work". Hunting trips and other social events are mentioned, indicating that the garrison must have been well established and secure. Evidently the risk of attack by the Scots must have been low. One tablet enumerates the strength of the garrison and refers to six wounded soldiers, but does not specify whether they were injured in combat or by accident. Another tablet, which may have been a report from a spy, states: "the Britons are unprotected by armour. There are very many cavalry. The cavalry do not use swords nor do the wretched Britons mount in order to throw javelins."

The handwriting on the tablets shows the development of cursive script, along with poor punctuation and, perhaps not surprisingly, bad spelling and the frequent use of slang. Some of the tablets are blank: although they may simply have been unused, it is also possible that they contain secret messages written in invisible ink. Some texts are in a form of shorthand which has still not been deciphered.

At the end of the occupation there seems to have been an attempt to burn the tablets, perhaps when the garrison was withdrawing for duties elsewhere, but fortunately rain put the fire out and a layer of mud was washed over them.

The historical background

We know quite a lot about the Roman invasion of the British Isles in 43 AD and the first 40 years of the occupation thanks to the historian Tacitus. His interest was stimulated and informed by his father-in-law Agricola, the provincial governor of Britain who finally overcame the Caledonian tribes in the north in 82–3 AD, before being recalled to Rome. Tacitus complained that "Britain was subjugated and immediately let slip". The Romans withdrew from Scotland and drew a line from Carlisle to the Tyne–Solway isthmus marked by the Stanegate Road, which was fortified with a series of garrisons such as Vindolanda.

Above: The original wooden fortress of Vindolanda was rebuilt several times and finally replaced with more durable stone. Excavation has revealed the lower parts of the buildings, but much of the original stonework was removed in the centuries after the fort was abandoned by the Romans.

A NATION DIVIDED
Civil War Battlefields, USA

The battlefields are monuments to a bloody civil war that cost at least 620,000 lives, but gave freedom to 3.5 million slaves.

The American Civil War, which rumbled across so much of this vast country from 1861 until 1865, has generated more detailed research than almost any other conflict in history, and continues to provide a grim fascination for many Americans today and a source of continuing argument for experts. Military historians and archaeologists have combined to recover and reconstruct the often complex and fast-moving events and manoeuvres of the campaigns along with the main "players", especially those that were spectacularly successful such as Lee, Jackson, Meade, Grant, and Sherman.

The catastrophic sundering of the still young United States into two nations in 1861 ended up costing more than 620,000 lives, by far the biggest loss in American history relative to the total population of the time (more than 31 million).

The causes

In 1858 Abraham Lincoln, upon accepting the Republican nomination for a seat in the Senate, predicted: "A house divided against itself cannot stand. I believe this government cannot endure, permanently half slave and half free ... It will become one thing or the other."

Lincoln's election to the presidency in 1860 was followed by South Carolina's secession from the Union, which followed by ten other southern states, formed the Confederacy, with its capital at Richmond, Virginia. Lincoln's main objective was the maintenance of a system of free labour which was under threat from the growth of slave labour for the westward expansion of a cotton-based agriculture. In all the seceding states the populations included 25 per cent or more people of African or Caribbean origin, unlike the rest of the country where the proportion was much lower. Lincoln wanted to preserve the Union and he wanted the seceding states back in the fold with their institutions intact; only later did he reluctantly support the emancipation of slaves. The emancipation proclamation became effective on 1 January 1863, but preserved slavery in states that were loyal to the Union.

The reality of war

Upon declaration of war, many young men eagerly joined up, often spurred on by their womenfolk and families, and under the impression that it would be a grand adventure, quickly resolved – within 90 days was the general opinion. The keen volunteers got more than they bargained for. Even by July 1861 and the first battle of Bull Run, the initial enthusiasm and idealism were soured by the reality of the conflict. But it was not until June 1862, when General Robert E. Lee took charge of the Confederate Army of Northern Virginia and pushed the Federal Army back from Richmond, that the nature of the conflict changed. Lee had the best part of a year's success in the east, and it became a protracted and bloody war in which many innocent civilians died and many of the militiary victims perished from disease and infected wounds. The initial promise of romantic dashing cavalry and individual heroism descended into a much more modern type of warfare which

---

Key Facts: Civil War Battlefields

Location: Eastern half of USA; more than 10,000 recorded, of which some 400 are considered worthy of protection

Date: 1861–5

Display: Some on site, see websites for detailed information

such as: www.nationalgeographic.com/magazine/0504 and www.americancivilwar.com

presaged that of World War I. Mechanization with railroads, armoured warships, submarines, mines, repeating rifles, rifled barrels, telegraphic communications, entrenched positions, and slow attrition with mass slaughter took over and ground both sides down. The bloodiest days in American history, 16–18 September 1862, saw 23,000 killed at Antietam in Maryland. The sheer firepower and greater resources, especially a continuing supply of new combatants, won the day for the Federal Army.

With the benefit of hindsight, the Federal forces were bound to win in the long run. Their eventual control of all major waterways, lines of communication, and transport (especially the mechanized railroads), as well as their growing industrial might, was inexorable. Nevertheless, the Confederate Army under the inspired leadership of General Robert E. Lee won significant victories, defeating a succession of Federal generals and carrying the day. By the late summer of 1862 Confederate fortunes were at their high point, but within a year the tide was turning and the major turning points were the battle of Vicksburg in the western theatre and that of Gettysburg in the eastern theatre. Both took place in July 1863.

Vicksburg

By late 1862 it was realized that control of the great Mississippi River was vital to the prosecution of the war. If the Federal forces could control the river they could pretty well prevent the three westernmost Confederate states of Texas, Arkansas, and Louisiana from feeding the war with recruits and supplies. However, the city of Vicksburg, the biggest in the state of Mississippi, commanded the river from its site 480 km (300 miles) upriver from the sea and strategically perched on a 61-m (200-ft) high bluff on the east bank. At the end of October 1862, Major General Ulysses S. Grant

Above: **Bloody lane, a road at Antietam Creek, near Sharpsburg, Maryland, was the scene of the bloodiest fighting of the Civil War in September 1862. Over 23,000 men died in the battle, 5,000 on the lane alone.**

Above: **The American Civil War was one of the first modern wars to use entrenched lines to try and consolidate or solidify strategic military positions, especially those in open ground which would otherwise be very vulnerable to intensive small arms and cannon fire.**

faced the daunting task of capturing Vicksburg and completing Federal control of all navigable waterways. Grant was a graduate of Westpoint and a veteran of the Mexican War, but had quit the army before the Civil War broke out. He was 39 when he joined the federal forces, and with his experience was quickly promoted as he notched up several notable victories at Fort Henry and Fort Donaldson, the latter including the taking of 14,000 prisoners. By April 1862 he was again promoted, this time to Major General, and added the bloody battle of Shiloh to his list, but by this time he realized that the war was going to be one of protracted struggle and mortal combat requiring the successive destruction of Confederate armies.

The problems Vicksburg posed for Grant were several. It was deep in enemy territory and initially without supply lines. It commanded the river approaches, and all the approaches from the west were across waterlogged ground and the eastern approaches were heavily defended. For Lieutenant General John C. Pemberton, in command of the defence, the problem was one of supplies of food, munitions, and men.

Grant took his time and tried a number of approaches before successfully running the gauntlet of the defences by river at night with Rear Admiral David D. Porter. Relieving Confederate

forces of some 32,000 under the command of Joseph E. Johnston, who had been the saviour at Bull Run, this time arrived too late to save Vicksburg. On 4 July 1863 Pemberton surrendered and Grant took nearly 31,000 prisoners, 170 cannon, and 60,000 rifles. Although the campaign had cost Grant 10,000 dead, this was less than half the 23,000 Federal casualties at Gettysburg in the eastern theatre, which was the other turning point in the Civil War. Still, the final surrender did not take place until April 1865.

Gettysburg

With the death of General Thomas J. "Stonewall" Jackson in May 1863 from wounds received during their victorious campaign at Chancellorsville, Lee's Confederate forces had to be quickly reorganized and revitalized. Lee moved north across the Potomac into Pennsylvania to lift the unremitting pressure on Virginia and the capital, Richmond. On the way Lee and his forces had to endure a large and brutal cavalry engagement at Brandy Station on 9 June which was inconclusive. But Lee's infantry were the decided victors at the second battle of Winchester (14–15 June), and by 1 July the opposing forces were yet again brought together at the crossroads town of Gettysburg. Initially, the battle went well for Lee, but the newly

Right: Archaelogists walk past a series of trenches which were abandoned at the end of World War I near the northern Belgian city of Ypres. The battle here in 1915 is notorious for marking the first use of poison gas in the War.

appointed Federal commander General George Gordon Meade managed to hold on to their hilltop position despite being virtually surrounded. Desperate Confederate assaults on the position very nearly succeeded, but ultimately they failed to grasp the advantage when they held it. The final Confederate attempt on 3 July, known as "Pickett's Charge", was a murderous affair for both sides and ended in failure for the Confederates. Each side lost around 25,000 men in the Civil War's largest battle.

Lee's army retreated towards the Potomac River during the night of the 4–5 July. Despite being pursued by Meade, they managed to cross back into Virginia. Although he had won the battle, Meade was criticized for not capturing the rest of Lee's forces and shortening the war. As it was, the conflict continued for another two years, with huge losses of life.

The battle of Gettysburg in early July 1863 proved to be a turning point in the war, but it was not until 9 April 1865 that Lee surrendered to Grant at Appomattox Court House; on 26 April General Joseph E. Johnston surrendered to General William T. Sherman at Durham Station. Some Confederates fought on until the beginning of June and, finally, the Confederate cruiser CSS *Shenandoah* surrendered in Liverpool to British officials on 6 November 1865.

Battlefield Archaeology

Historically, battlefield archaeology has concentrated on fortifications and other constructions. With many relatively modern conflicts from the American Civil War onwards, the exact location of battlefields is quite well documented, although details may not be so clear. Archaeological investigation using a variety of techniques including non-invasive geophysical procedures and even remote sensing, plus excavation (as at the illustrated World War I battlefield of Ypres), restoration, and even reconstruction are all used as part of new interpretation and education programmes linked to individual sites.

Battlefield research can focus on various apsects such as the recovery of artefacts ranging from cartridge and shell cases to bullets and the remains of gun emplacements, often with the use of metal detectors and local enthusiasts. Analysis of such remains can help the identification of weapons used which may conflict with written accounts and help resolve arguments over which side had the advntage in terms of equipment and supplies of ammunition.

Such investigation showed how native americans outgunned and out manouvered General George Custer's Seventh Cavalry in the 1876 battle of Little Bighorn. Thousands of artefacts and some skeletal material has been recovered and computer analysis of their distribution demonstrated what weapons were used and how the terrain was used to advantage by the Sioux and Cheyenne. The site in southeastern Montana is now a National Monument.

PRIDE OF THE ENGLISH FLEET
Portsmouth, England

Henry VIII's flagship, the *Mary Rose*, sank more than 400 years ago. Now raised and restored, it is the only 16th-century warship in the world on public display.

The *Mary Rose*, King Henry VIII's favourite and one-time flagship and pride of the English navy, went to the bottom of the Solent, off Portsmouth, during a battle with the French fleet on 19 July 1545. Most of the crew were lost, along with Vice Admiral George Carew and Captain Roger Grenville. It would be 437 years before the vessel re-emerged from the murky waters.

A catastrophe unfolds

The events leading up to the sinking began when the French sent a fleet of 200 ships to destroy the much smaller English fleet and invade the Isle of Wight. The English king and many of his courtiers were in Portsmouth to witness the battle; tents had been put up on the quayside. On the evening of 18 July, Henry dined on his new flagship, *Henry Grace a Dieu*, with Admiral Viscount Lisle and Sir George Carew, his newly appointed vice admiral who later returned to his ship, the *Mary Rose*.

Calm seas the following morning gave the French galleys an advantage over the English ships. What actually happened to the *Mary Rose* is not entirely clear. The French claimed to have sunk her with cannon fire, but a survivor's account tells a different story. Apparently, the vessel heeled when the sails were raised and caught a gust of wind. Water poured into the hull through the lowest gunports, which were only about 1.2 m (4 ft) above the waterline and had been left open after firing. The inrush of

water destabilized the vessel, causing it to heel further, loosing a heavy cascade of cannon balls. That, together with a shift in the ship's ballast, made the roll unstoppable. At least one cannon broke loose and fell onto some of the gun crew, trapping and crushing them. Their leather jerkins, boots, and bones were found beneath the cannon. Of the crew of more than 400, only 25 or 30 survived.

Less than a month later 30 salvage experts were brought in from Venice to attempt to raise the *Mary Rose*. They recovered the sails and attached ropes to the masts, but the foremast broke when they tried to right the vessel. They then tried to drag the wreck into shallower water, but when that failed the scheme was abandoned.

Raising the *Mary Rose*

In June 1836 a local fisherman snagged his nets on the wreck and appealed to pioneer diver John Deane. Using the first practical diving helmet, which he and his brother had invented, Deane freed the nets and, while doing so, found timbers and a bronze cannon. Over the next few years he recovered several iron guns, four bronze ones, and two longbows from the wreck.

In the mid 1960s, Alexander McKee and the British Sub-Aqua Club launched Project Solent Ships to investigate a number of wrecks off Portsmouth. In 1967, side-scan sonar revealed a hull-shaped outline submerged deep in mud. The following year further scans convinced McKee

Key Facts: The *Mary Rose*

Location: The Solent, Hampshire, England	**Explored by:** The Mary Rose Committee led by Mary Rule
Age: 16th century	**Display:** Portsmouth, Hampshire, southern England
Discovered: First in 1836 by John Deaneagain in 1967 by Alexander McKee	

Right: The remains of the wooden hull of the *Mary Rose*, which had been preserved in the mud of Portsmouth harbour, were surrounded and supported by a steel cradle before being lifted from the water in 1982 and placed in a specially built dock for long-term preservation.

Left: One of the *Mary Rose*'s iron cannon being lifted from the muds of the Solent in which it had been preserved for well over 400 years. However, careful treatment is required to preserve such metal objects once they have been exposed to the air.

that they had found the 422-year-old wreck.
The Mary Rose Committee was then formed by
McKee, archaeologist Mary Rule, Lieutenant
Commander Alan Bax, and W.O.B. Majer. With
very little money, a team of volunteers ranging
from London taxi drivers to professional divers
methodically probed the mud of the seabed.
Known as Mad Mac's Marauders, they operated
from small boats in strong tidal currents and
practically zero visibility under water.

In the winter of 1968 they confirmed
submerged solids, then used water jets and a
dredger to remove mud and silt. Loose timbers
were recovered, then an iron gun. On 5 May 1971
Percy Ackland spotted the timber frame of the
Mary Rose protruding from the mud. A further
27,000 dives yielded a vast range of finds: timbers
and ropes, archers' wooden bows, food, and the
skeletons of many of those on board that fateful

day in 1545. Much of the recovered material had
been well preserved under thick layers of mud.

Mounting publicity, together with the
enthusiasm of Prince Charles for the project,
enabled the salvage crew to raise the funds needed
to recover the entire wreck. The lifting operation
was long, expensive, and tricky, but eventually in
1982 the surviving starboard timbers of the hull
reappeared from the Solent.

Centrepiece of a new fleet

The *Mary Rose* was built between 1509 and 1511,
soon after Henry VIII's accession to the throne.
With a keel length of 32 m (105 ft), a waterline
length of 38.5 m (126 ft), a breadth of 11.66 m
(38 ft 3 in), and a draught of 4.6 m (15 ft), the
ship was small by modern standards. Its weight
increased significantly over time from 500 tons
in 1527 when first refitted in Portsmouth, to 700

tons when refitted again in the Thames around 1536. These refits included considerable strengthening of the hull, which had innovative carvel planking, rather than being clinkered like most earlier ships.

On becoming king, Henry VIII inherited a fleet of no more than five ships. In time of war his navy was supplemented by merchant vessels which were equipped with guns and as many archers as could be accommodated on board. When England was threatened by Scotland and France, Henry determined to expand and upgrade the Royal Navy. The new carvel hull design allowed water-tight gunports to be fitted to accommodate heavier guns, which had to be positioned as low to the waterline as possible for stability.

The *Mary Rose* carried an impressive range of armaments, from heavy cannon (both bronze and iron) to swivel guns, handguns, pikes, archers' longbows, and personal weapons from sailors' knives to officers' swords. Some 137 longbows and 3500 arrows have been recovered.

Construction of the vessel is not well documented, but there is indirect evidence that four new ships were built in 1509 and further documents from 1510 suggest that the *Mary Rose* and another vessel, the *Peter Pomegranate*, were built at Portsmouth. A lot of money was spent in 1511 on equipping the king's new ships with "flags, banners, and streamers" – the *Mary Rose* was the flagship and pride of the new fleet.

The crew

In 1545 the crew consisted of 200 sailors, 185 soldiers, and 30 gunners. When recovered, the remains of some 200 were found. Most of the victims were fit young men, but there were also a few boys and men in their forties. Their average height was just 1.7 m (5 ft 7½ in) – normal for the male population of northwestern Europe at the time. Their monthly pay had been raised in January 1545 from 5 shillings to 6 shillings and 8 pence.

The *Vasa*'s first and last voyage

The story of the *Mary Rose* has much in common with that of the 17th-century *Vasa*, the new flagship of King Gustav of Sweden.

With a length of more than 60 m (200 ft) and displacement of 1210 tons, the *Vasa* was the biggest ship of its time. It was potentially top-heavy – the upper hull carried three masts, 10 sails, and 64 bronze cannon – but the designers thought that they had counterbalanced the enormous weight above deck with 122 tons of stone that were stowed in the hold as ballast.

But the designers had miscalculated, with disastrous consequences. On its maiden voyage in 1628, the ship was just 1300 m (4300 ft) out from her berth in Stockholm harbour, well in sight of land, when a squall suddenly blew up. The ship keeled over, water flowed in through open gunports, and the vessel quickly capsized and sank, taking with it most of its crew of 133 sailors, plus various visiting dignitaries who were on board for the occasion. Decades later, in 1664, a primitive diving bell was used to recover some of the ship's valuable bronze cannon.

Luckily for archaeologists, the *Vasa* sank into cold, muddy, and brackish water, which preserved many of her timbers and artefacts. The *Vasa* was rediscovered in 1956 and brought back to the surface in 1961, 333 years after it had gone down. Some 30 years of painstaking conservation saved about 95 per cent of the ship's original timber. The vessel is now open to public viewing at the Vasa Museum, Stockholm.

DEATH OF THE *BISMARCK*
Denmark Strait, North Atlantic Ocean

With its awesome power and speed, the *Bismarck* seemed invincible and posed a terrible threat to Allied shipping. The British had to sink it no matter what the cost.

The Bismark

EUROPE

The active-service career of the World War II German battleship *Bismarck* was short but eventful. In its first engagement it sank an icon of the British Royal Navy – HMS *Hood* – with the loss of almost everyone on board. The subsequent naval engagement was to be one of the war's most ferocious.

Predator on the high seas

The *Bismarck* was launched by Adolf Hitler on 14 February 1939. It carried eight 15-inch guns and was capable of speeds of 30 knots. More ominously for a world on the threshold of conflict, it displaced 50,000 tons, in defiance of international law which limited battleships to 35,000 tons. This was a challenge to every country, and particularly to Britain, which at the time was the world's greatest maritime power.

The *Bismarck*'s big guns enabled it to engage an enemy at a range of 20 km (12 miles), and the ship was fast enough to outrun any of the British fleet. After the outbreak of war in September 1939 the *Bismarck* first went into hiding in a Norwegian fjord, but in 1941, escorted by the heavy cruiser *Prinz Eugen*, it slipped out into the North Atlantic, where its commander intended to attack merchant shipping bringing vital supplies to England.

The British were notified of the movement by the Norwegian Resistance, and shortly afterwards the two German warships were spotted by an RAF reconnaissance Spitfire. The Royal Navy gave chase with several vessels, including the veteran battleship HMS *Hood* (launched in 1920) and two

new cruisers, HMS *Norfolk* and *Suffolk*. On 24 May they sighted the German ships in the Denmark Strait between Iceland and Greenland.

The ensuing engagement was disastrous for the British: the *Bismarck*'s fifth salvo destroyed the *Hood*. It sank quickly, and only three of its crew of 1413 survived. The *Bismarck* then sped away and the British lost track of it until they intercepted a radio message in which German Admiral Lutjens reported its position to Hitler.

Air attack – then the final battle

Once the Royal Navy re-established contact with the *Bismarck*, Swordfish biplanes from the aircraft carrier HMS *Ark Royal* managed to damage the German ship's steering gear with a torpedo. This slowed the *Bismarck* and enabled the British flagship HMS *King George V* and the battleship HMS *Nelson* to arrive on the scene as dusk fell on 26 May 1941. Rather than risk a night-time battle, Admiral Tovey waited until 0849 the following morning before giving the order to open fire at a range of 20,000 m (12 miles).

With the *Bismarck*'s rudders jammed hard to port and unable to manoeuvre, the outcome was inevitable. But still the German warship proved hard to sink. Firing its last salvo at 0931, the *Bismarck* remained afloat despite sustaining repeated hits at point-blank range. It was not until 10.22 am that the ship finally rolled over and sank after having again been torpedoed. Although many of the surviving crew made it alive into the water and some of them were picked

---

Key Facts: The *Bismarck*

Location: 4790 m (15,700 ft) deep in the North Atlantic, 960 km (600 miles) west of Brest

Age: 1941

Discovered: In 1989 by Robert Ballard

Explored by: Robert Ballard

Display: www.kbismarck.com

up by the British ships, a possible sighting of submarines in the area forced the Royal Navy to break off any further rescue efforts. Of the *Bismarck*'s crew of 2221, all but 115 were lost.

Two wrecks, two graves

The wreck of the Bismarck was located and surveyed by American ocean scientist Robert Ballard on 8 June 1989 at a depth of 4790 m (15,700 ft) in international waters. Surprisingly much of the hull is intact, lying upright on the seabed, but deeply embedded in mud. The wreck site has been declared an official war grave by the Federal Republic of Germany.

On 20 July 2001 the remains of HMS *Hood* were discovered by David L. Mearns of Blue Water Recoveries. Subsequent investigation of the wreck confirmed that the aft magazine of the ship had been hit by an enemy shell and exploded. The bows had broken off after it sank.

Above: **The German World War II battleship *Bismarck*, which displaced 50,000 tons, was the largest and most technically sophisticated warship afloat. It was sunk by the Royal Navy in 1941. The hulk, discovered in 1989, is surprisingly intact, lying nearly 5 km (3 miles) down on the North Atlantic seabed.**

6

MIGRATION & COLONIZATION

Since the very beginnings of humankind, our ancestors have undertaken journeys – originally out of Africa and into Asia, and later into Europe and Australasia, then the New World, and, finally, throughout the Pacific. It is not known what has instilled this unique wanderlust in our species, and in many of the earlier cases we can only speculate how the journeys across water were undertaken. But archaeology has provided much intriguing evidence for early migrations, although it is not always clear whether people were invading or colonizing, or whether they were simply indulging in commerce, with influences and ideas moving around along with trade goods.

Because Asia and Europe are joined to Africa, it is impossible to find out exactly when people first migrated into them. But for other parts of the world to which access required the crossing of ocean, archaeology has been able to come up with some answers.

It will never be known when our ancestors first managed to traverse water on a simple craft, but currently it seems that *Homo erectus* must have done this: discoveries of his crude stone tools on the Indonesian island of Flores from around 800,000 years ago – which, even during periods of the lowest sea level, required at least two sea crossings, the first being of 25 km (15.5. miles) – not only imply that he could safely negotiate water barriers, but also that he had language, in view of the organization needed to build such craft.

Be that as it may, we also know from archaeological finds in northern Australia that people were already present there by around 60,000 years ago – it is difficult to be sure, as this date falls at the very limit of the radiocarbon method. The burials of Lake Mungo, discovered in southeastern Australia, seem to date back at least 40 or 50,000 years, indicating the rapid spread of people throughout that vast country.

On the other hand, the period when the New World was first colonized by humans is still a matter of hot debate, as is the route by which people arrived there. Most scholars still believe that they arrived from northeastern Asia via the Bering Strait, at a time when it formed a land bridge, but many are now beginning to consider routes across the Pacific or even the Atlantic. Although the orthodox view is still that people first entered North America around 15,000 years ago or later, there is a steadily growing body of solid evidence from Central and South America which points to a human presence long before then – certainly by 30,000 years ago, and perhaps even as far back as the time when people also entered Australia.

But regardless of when the New World was originally colonized, when was it first encountered by Europeans? The traditional view that Columbus discovered the Americas in 1492 AD was long challenged by rumours and beliefs that others, and especially the Vikings, had beaten him to it, but solid evidence was lacking – until the discovery of L'Anse aux Meadows in 1960. This settlement, together with others in Greenland, not only demonstrated the Vikings' prowess at maritime exploration, but also provided a classic example of untenable colonization – circumstances had prevented a permanent settlement in these areas, and the occupations were shortlived. Other cases of this kind can be seen elsewhere in the archaeological record, such as on some Pacific islands – for example, Pitcairn, which had been occupied by prehistoric Polynesians, but who had vanished when the *Bounty* mutineers arrived there at the end of the 18th century AD. Easter Island itself (see p. 106) might well have become another example of an abandoned settlement – or an extinct population – if the Europeans had not turned up and changed its history.

Where the Pacific islands are concerned, it took centuries for the ancient Polynesians – the greatest seafarers in the world – to colonize the whole vast area, and we shall never know how many voyages (whether planned or accidental) failed; however, it is likely that many canoes never returned home for a wide variety of reasons. Colonization is by no means always a straightforward enterprise, and this continues to be true today: countless desperate people still perish on the crude makeshift watercraft with which they attempt to escape their countries or seek refuge in another. And even the most modern technology is not immune to disaster – many of the passengers on the "unsinkable" *Titanic* were leaving the Old World to start a new life in America, never imagining that their possessions were destined to become archaeological specimens, and a moving testimony to a great human tragedy.

BONES IN THE SAND
Lake Mungo, Australia

Bones and other finds at Lake Mungo not only shed light on the peopling of Australia, but also call into question theories of human evolution.

Lake Mungo, in New South Wales, Australia, proved to be the camping and burial place of some of the oldest known occupants of that continent, dating to between 40,000 and 15,000 years ago. Traces of camp sites with stone tools, freshwater mussel shells, and animal and fish bones have been detected; however, the site is best known for the remains of more than 100 individuals. Many are fragmentary, but they also include an almost complete skeleton, and the world's oldest known cremation.

The Willandra Lakes, a series of inter-connecting lakes in the arid part of southwestern New South Wales, have been dry for the past 15,000 years, but at times before that they were filled with fresh water. In 1968, Australian geomorphologist Jim Bowler was studying the local climatic history when he noticed some burnt bones eroding out of a large crescent-shaped dune on the eastern shore of the former lake (some of the spectacular dunes here are known as the Walls of China).

Mungo woman

The sediments around the bones were removed as a block and excavated in the laboratory by physical anthropologist Alan Thorne. They proved to be the remains of a young woman (WLH 1), about 19 years of age, who had been buried about 26,000 years ago, according to initial dating. The body had been burned, then the bones were smashed into small pieces and burned in a small depression. Nearby there were 15 circular or oval patches of black deposit, which are the remnants of shallow hearths or ovens up to 1 m (just over 3 ft) across. These contained fragmented charcoal, burnt and broken animal and fish bones, fragments of emu eggshell, mussel shells, and sometimes stone tools. The emu eggs point to occupation in the autumn and winter, as the eggs are laid between April and November.

It was found that the young woman was short and light-boned – so gracile that muscle markings on the bones, even the skull, are barely perceptible. The skull is oval in shape, with a rounded forehead and small teeth and brow-ridges. In 1992, at a formal ceremony at Mungo, the remains of WLH 1 were returned to the custody of local Aboriginal groups, who stored them securely in a temporary keeping place.

Mungo man – or woman?

In 1974 Bowler discovered an older and far more complete skeleton 0.5 km (⅓ mile) to the east, after it was exposed by heavy rainfall. Initially dated to about 30,000 years, this adult male (WLH 3), about 50 years of age and around 1.7 m (5 ft 6 in) tall, had been buried on his side, with his hands crossed over the pelvis and powdered red ochre (from sources 30 km/19 miles away) scattered over him. He had chronic osteoarthritis in his right elbow, which must have caused considerable suffering during the latter part of his life. An unusual form of wear on the teeth suggests that he may have used them for stripping plant fibres for cords and

netting. Some specialists have argued that this individual may actually be a female.

Lakeside life

The camp sites around the lakes have yielded remains of fish, frogs, mussels, and crayfish from the lakes. The fish bones come primarily from one species, the golden perch, and all are of roughly the same size, which suggests that the people probably fished with nets. They also hunted wallabies, wombats, and native cats, as well as many small animals such as rat kangaroos and lizards. Food was cooked on fires or in earth ovens – at Mungo, one of the latter is 30,000 years old. These ovens were shallow pits, and contained ash, charcoal, and cooking stones; similar ovens are still used by Aborigines today.

Numerous stone tools were found, used mainly for chopping, cutting, and scraping. Microscopic traces on some of their edges showed that they had been used in scraping meat from bone and for cleaning plant tubers.

The first Australians

The Mungo finds revolutionized Australian prehistory. It was only in 1962, through excavations at Kenniff Cave, Queensland, that the first evidence emerged that the continent had been occupied in the last Ice Age. The Mungo finds not only pushed this back to 30,000 years, but also revealed something of the ceremonial life at that time. Since then, several sites have emerged which suggest an initial colonization of Australia as long as 60,000 years ago in the Northern

Above: **Part of the spectacular formations known as the Walls of China, along the eastern shore of dried-up Lake Mungo.**

Territory. The date is important because Australia was never joined to Southeast Asia, so any journey to Australia by these early people required a sea voyage of at least 35 miles (50 km), which again points to their technological capabilities.

Dating the finds

The human remains found at Mungo raised some interesting questions because the people here seemed to have more delicate features than living Aborigines. In 1967 some skeletons were found at Kow Swamp, Victoria, dating to between 13,000 and 9500 years ago. These remains – representing at least 40 men, women, and children – were far more rugged and robust than the Mungo people, despite being more recent. Normally, robust forms are older than gracile forms. As the Kow Swamp finds were somewhat similar to more ancient fossils from Java, while the Mungo ones closely resembled Chinese finds, it was proposed by Thorne and others that there had been at least two separate migrations of people to Australia from different parts of Southeast Asia, but this idea remains highly controversial. Other specialists have stressed the diversity of Aboriginal remains, and some have suggested that some features of the Kow Swamp skulls can be explained as the result of the practice of binding the heads of infants.

In the mid 1980s, improved radiocarbon techniques pushed the date of WLH 3 back to at least 38,000 years; then in 1999 Thorne announced a new age for the skeleton of between 68,000 and 56,000 years, based on other dating techniques (electron spin resonance, uranium series, and optical stimulated luminescence analyses). However, this dating has proved to be extremely controversial. Bowler himself, for example, has carried out new analyses in recent years which indicate that WLH 3 – and also the Mungo woman – date to around 40,000 years ago, and stone tools at the site have been dated to 50,000 years.

Evidence from genes

More recently, DNA has been abstracted from WLH 3 – the oldest ever extracted from human remains, with the permission of local Aboriginal people. It has been found to contain an extinct genetic sequence that does not occur in modern human populations, despite its owner being anatomically modern.

This poses a problem in the domain of human evolution. Specialists who support the "Out of Africa" theory maintain that all living peoples are descended from a group of fully modern *Homo sapiens* who left Africa about 150,000 to 100,000 years ago; they and their descendants spread around the world, replacing existing populations of archaic people such as Neanderthals and the more ancient *Homo erectus*. However, those specialists who support the alternative "regional continuity" believe that, ever since *Homo erectus* began migrating out of Africa more than 1.5 million years ago, there has been a single evolving species, and early humans shared their genes through interbreeding.

The DNA analysis is troubling for the "Out of Africa" model because it points to an earlier exodus from Africa if the early Mungo date were correct. According to the Regional Continuity model, Aborigines are descended from two different groups of *Homo sapiens* – as mentioned above, an early gracile group from China, and a later robust group from Java – who landed in Australia 40,000 years apart and interbred, but not all genes were passed on to future generations.

Another, quite different facet of the Mungo dates is that they may help shed light on the disappearance of the Australian megafauna. Evidence that people spread rapidly across Australia around 50,000 years ago is taken by some to support the "blitzkrieg" theory of the extinction of the continent's large mammals shortly after the arrival of humans, whereas other researchers have argued that climate change may have been to blame.

MIGRATION & COLONIZATION – **BONES IN THE SAND**   155

THE PEOPLE WHO BEAT COLUMBUS
L'Anse aux Meadows, Canada

A Newfoundland site is the earliest known European settlement in the New World, having been founded by those great adventurers, the Vikings, around 1000 AD.

During the 9th and 10th centuries AD, the Vikings spread through Europe, into Russia, and across the Atlantic. They reached Iceland in the mid 9th century and Greenland 50 years later. Two Icelandic sagas told of the discovery, settlement, and final abandonment of a territory known as Vinland. Was Vinland North America, and had there been a Norse settlement there?

Searching for Vikings

The Norwegian writer and explorer Helge Ingstad set out to find archaeological evidence to verify the sagas. In 1960 he was searching for evidence of Norse landing places along the rocky, indented, and island-strewn northeast coast of Canada. A vast rocky promontory forms a northern arm of the island of Newfoundland and stretches north towards the Labrador coast. Here only the narrow Straits of Belle Isle separate the island from the mainland. With its relative proximity to the Viking settlements of southern Greenland this was an obvious possibility as a landfall site for any Vikings who were either purposefully searching for new territories and resources, or were driven off course by storms.

The Vikings may have chosen the site because there were fewer Native Americans – whose weaponry and skills at warfare equalled those of the Norsemen – here than on the mainland. A Norse coin minted between 1065 and 1080 AD was found in a Native American occupation site on the coast of Maine, along with Inuit type stone artefacts derived from Labrador. The coin is probably evidence that the Norsemen reached Labrador (known as Markland to the Vikings) and traded with the Inuit, who then traded it with Native Americans to the south.

At L'Anse aux Meadows, local inhabitant George Decker drew Ingstad's attention to a cluster of overgrown grassy humps. Over the next eight years Helge, with his archaeologist wife, Anne Stine Ingstad, and an international team of experts, carefully excavated the site.

The comforts of home

They found that the ridges were the remains of the walls of eight multi-roomed Viking buildings (up to 25 m/82 ft long) with designs very similar to those used in Greenland and Iceland around 1000 AD Both the low walls and massive roof were made of earth and grass sods laid over a frame of timber. With some modifications the technique was used for centuries throughout Scandinavia and Viking territories elsewhere. The buildings can weather even the fiercest Atlantic storms.

A long, narrow fireplace was constructed in the middle of the floor where the pitch of the roof was at its highest. The hearth served as heating, lighting, and stove, with the fumes rising into the roof where fish and other meat (when available) were hung and preserved by the smoke.

The identity of the builders was clinched by the discovery of certain artefacts. A bronze ring-headed pin of the kind used by Norse people to fasten their cloaks was found in the hearth. And there was a small fragment of brass that had once

Key Facts: L'Anse aux Meadows

Location: Northern Newfoundland, Canada

Age: Around 1000 AD

Discovered: In 1960 by Helge Ingstad

Explored by: Ingstad and international team of archaeologists

Display: Reconstructions of three Norse buildings can be visited, and there are exhibits of the Viking lifestyle, along with artefacts and information about the discovery of the site

been a gilded ornament. Other finds were a small spindle whorl used as a flywheel for hand spinning, a single glass bead, a fragment of a bone needle possibly for knitting, and a whetstone for sharpening needles and knives. Traditionally these latter were female belongings, and it would seem that the settlers included both men and women, and may have numbered as many as 100 people.

In addition, slag was found along with many iron boat nails, showing that iron had been smelted and worked for the repair and perhaps the building of boats. The style of the nails again confirmed the Norse identity of the site.

Canadian Park authorities made further investigations from 1973 to 1976. In a peat bog just below the settlement archaeologists found three layers of wood debris, one of which related to the Norse settlement. It consisted of chippings and shavings from woodworking, with metal tools and a few broken objects such as a broken floorboard from a small Viking boat. Altogether it is evidence that the site was used primarily as winter quarters for boat repairs, with both carpenters and metalworkers. Here Viking ships

could be beached and refitted for the long and dangerous homeward journey to Greenland and perhaps further to Iceland.

Butternuts: crucial clues

The discovery of butternuts at L'Anse aux Meadows site also provides evidence for further foraging trips along the northeastern seaboard, perhaps as far south as New Brunswick and the St Lawrence River. Butternuts do not grow in Newfoundland and have a northern limit in northeastern New Brunswick which was also the growth limit for wild grapes. During the summer months some of the Norsemen voyaged south looking for new resources, and probably it was the discovery of wild grapes that was the origin of the Vinland mentioned in the Norse sagas. Others stayed at L'Anse aux Meadows collecting food and fuel, and making nails for their boats.

During the autumn the voyagers returned to overwinter at the Newfoundland site before they all departed back to Greenland. The absence of middens (rubbish dumps) suggests that the site was not occupied for very long.

Above: **The interior of a reconstructed dwelling at L'Anse aux Meadows shows a typical Viking-style windowless wooden construction in which a whole family would have lived. with lows walls, a high-pitched roof, and central hearth.**

IN SEARCH OF THE *TITANIC*
Grand Banks, North Atlantic Ocean

The *Titanic* was the largest and most opulent liner of her day when she sank in 1912 with great loss of life. Some 70 years later, a group of explorers set out to find her.

At 11.40pm on Sunday, 14 April 1912, RMS *Titanic* was steaming at 20 knots for New York on her maiden voyage from Southampton. Lookout Fred Fleet spotted an iceberg 500 yards dead ahead. Soon after, the liner was sliced open below the waterline by the berg, and within 2½ hours the largest ship of its day had sunk, drowning 1522 people.

Rumours and facts

The *Titanic* became an icon almost immediately after she sank. The tragedy was headline news around the world, and her sinking came to be seen as some sort of omen – as the end of an era, that of the British empire with all its wealth, pride, and opulence.

It seemed as if everyone had something to say about the sinking, or a story to tell. Why had the ship sunk, and why had none of the several ships in the neighbourhood seen her distress rockets or heard the distress calls? There were tales of the stoical gallantry of many of the crew and passengers, and stories of cowardice, too.

And then there was the matter of the lifeboats. The lifeboat capacity was only 1178, although there were 2227 passengers and crew on board. Captain Edward J. Smith, who knew that there would be more than 1000 people left behind if she sank, made the decision to go down with his command. Rich and poor died together in the icy waters; among the dead were multimillionaire John Jacob Astor, as well as many impoverished steerage passengers.

A needle in a haystack

Finding the *Titanic* at the bottom of the North Atlantic would always be a romantic pipedream without vast improvements in underwater technology and knowledge about the oceans. French and American marine scientists pioneered the exploration of the depths of the world's oceans following the end of World War II. There were compelling economic, strategic defence, and scientific reasons for investigating the last great unknown region of the earth. By the 1980s the scientific goal of mapping the ocean floor had been achieved. This sparked a revolution in our understanding of how ocean basins had formed, encapsulated in the theory of plate tectonics.

The American marine geologist Dr Robert D. Ballard had been at the forefront of this work, which required new technology in the form of submersible craft. These vessels were strong enough to descend to great depths, yet manoeuvrable enough to explore the ocean floor.

Independently, French scientists such as Jean-Louis Michel had developed their own highly successful submersibles. As well, deep sonar imaging allowed the ocean floor to be scanned with sufficient detail to be able to spot objects as large as the *Titanic*. Technically, for the first time it had become possible to locate the wreck of the great ship. And yet, although the general location of the vessel's sinking was known – off the Grand Banks of Newfoundland – there was still a vast region of ocean floor to be searched.

Key Facts: RMS *Titanic*

Location: 530 km (350 miles) southeast of Newfoundland, Canada, at 3810 m (12,500 ft) depth

Age: Sunk 1912 on maiden voyage

Discovered: 1985 by Jean-Louis Michel and Robert Ballard

Explored by: Robert Ballard

Display: www.titanic-nautical.com and other websites

The search used sonar scanning. This requires very accurate navigation and thousands of nautical miles of sailing up and down carefully plotted and closely spaced survey lines at half-mile intervals, which allows an overlapping sonar map of the ocean floor to be constructed.

The *Titanic* is sighted

In July 1985 the French research vessel *Le Surtoit* began the sonar search and covered 70 per cent of the search area by the time it had to return to port. The *Knorr*, an American oceanographic research ship, took over. Ballard decided to look for debris from the *Titanic*, which he reasoned should cover a greater area than the vessel itself.

At 12.48 am on 1 September 1985, Stu Harris, one of Ballard's team, spotted some wreckage on a video monitor. The *Titanic* had been found at last, in 3810 m (12,500 ft) of water about 530 km (350 miles) southeast of Newfoundland. The bow and the stern were 600 m (2000 ft) apart, the ship having broken in two when it sank. Ballard returned in 1986 to document the shipwreck in more detail.

Top: The *Titanic* was the biggest passenger vessel of its day and was advertised as being unsinkable because of its technically sophisticated hull structure.

Middle: Corrosion in the cold, deep waters of the North Atlantic is slow, and the remaining metal structures of the hull are still remarkably well preserved.

Bottom: Stacks of the vessel's vast crockery store still lie where they fell from their storage racks, and are surprisingly intact.

7

SCIENCE AND ARCHAEOLOGY

As humans we seem to have an unique and insatiable fascination with our past. Our desire to uncover the truths of that past has strengthened over the past 200 years, as archaeology emerged as an increasingly scientific discipline. Today, the science of archaeology is developing more quickly than at any time in its history. Whole new areas of investigation have been opened up with new scientific understanding of subjects. For instance, forensic archaelogy uses genetics and biomolecules such as DNA. And new scientific technologies for dating ancient materials, the ultra-high magnification produced by electron microscopes, and the non-destructive three-dimensional imaging of hidden objects and materials, especially bone, have opened whole new windows on the past. Archaeology has re-emerged as one of the most popular and fascinating areas of investigation of the past. As a discipline its boundaries with history, earth, and biological science have become increasingly blurred, with spectacular results.

DNA Analysis

One of the most important developments in the science of archaeology has been founded upon the understanding of genetics through the discovery of the structure of DNA and more recently the technical ability to map whole genomes of different organisms from the humble yeast to that of humans.

Preserving DNA

Unfortunately, complex proteins such as DNA are very fragile and susceptible to rapid degradation following the death of the host animal or plant – generally within hours. However, there are certain conditions under which such proteins can survive. In exceptional circumstances, identifiable fragments of DNA many tens of thousands of years old can be recovered, but the hope of finding even older DNA is remote. In the 1980s, some of the first ancient DNA to be recovered came from an Egyptian mummy and the dried skin of the extinct zebra-like quagga, a few thousand years old. Since then there have been false claims that DNA has been obtained from insects embedded in amber, even amber that was formed tens of millions of years ago when the dinosaurs roamed the earth. But none of the results has been replicated, they are all the result of contamination by modern DNA – it only takes a bacterium or fleck of dandruff to give a misleading result. Some of the oldest DNA has been recovered from the tissues of mammoths some 70,000 years old frozen in Siberian permafrost.

Heat, light (or more particularly oxygen), and water are all harmful to the preservation of DNA, as is any microbial activity which is part of the normal decomposition process. So the best possible conditions are to be found in cold, dry, and dark environments – cave-floor deposits in high latitudes, burial on alpine peaks, or in freeze-drying environments such as ice and permafrost. Bone is a fairly tough material and good medium for the preservation of DNA, which is present within the organic collagen proteins which help to strengthen and bond the inorganic components of bone together. But bone is also porous and so needs to be entombed somehow or other in cool, dry, and dark conditions to give much chance of DNA preservation.

Testing theories

Of the ancient biomolecules recovered in recent decades, Neanderthal bone-derived DNA is the most interesting and important (see p. 164). Fragmental DNA some 40,000 years old, from the original 19th-century find in Germany has been compared with 29,000 year old bone DNA recovered from a Neanderthal child found some 4000 km (about 2500 miles) to the east in the northern Caucasus mountains. The identification of some distinct differences in the DNA not only supports the claim that the Neanderthals were a separate and extinct human species, but that they also seem to have had a common gene pool over a period of at least 50,000 years. Furthermore, as there is no sign of Neanderthal DNA in the modern European gene pool, the idea that Europeans might have descended from the Neanderthals has at last been laid to rest.

Some of the most exciting DNA-derived information has been recovered by sampling discrete modern populations and ethnic groups. Both mitochondrial DNA, derived solely through the maternal line, and analysis of markers on the male Y chromosome are revealing fascinating details about the movements of peoples and populations, and their inter-relationships around the world. Such information has helped settle long-running arguments such as the origination of native Americans from Siberia and disproved various fantasies, however appealing.

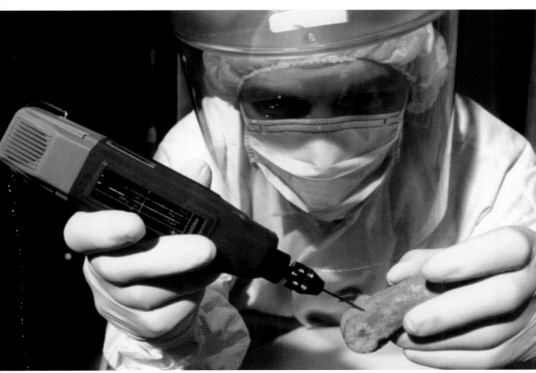

Above and left: A technician prepares a sample of bone from a fossil of a neanderthal human, *Homo sapiens neanderthalis*, for analysis of its DNA genetic material. It has been suggested that Neanderthals were the ancestors of modern Europeans. Comparisons of DNA extracted from Neanderthal fossils with modern DNA have shown that this is unlikely.

WE ARE WHAT WE EAT
Isotope Geochemistry

Certain types of food leave distinct chemical signatures in our bones and teeth (and those of other animals). Chemical analysis of fossil bones can indentify these traces (especially stable isotopes of carbon and nitrogen, but also ratios of strontium to calcium) and so the kind of food consumed over significant periods of time.

Opposite: A scientist uses forceps to extract pulp from a fossil tooth of the extinct North American mastodon *Mastodon americanus*. The pulp cavity of this tooth is scraped for tissue that may still contain fragments of DNA genetic material. DNA of mastodons and mammoths is then compared with living elephants, to establish their evolutionary links.

Carbon isotopes

Although the carbon isotopes 12 and 13 are present in the atmosphere in roughly equal proportions, plants incorporate differing amounts into their tissues during photosynthesis. In general, plants take on slightly more 12C than is present in the atmosphere. Trees, shrubs, and temperate grasses, however, incorporate less 13C (relative to 12C) into their tissues than tropical and savanna grasses (including maize). By contrast, ocean waters have a greater ratio of carbon 13 to carbon 12, and marine plant tissues reflect this. All terrestrial and marine organisms ultimately depend on plants for their life, so their original isotope signatures can be transferred up the food chain.

Analyzing isotope ratios from the bones of prehistoric communities can show us the extent to which they fed upon food from the sea or the land. For example, a study of successive Mesolithic, Neolithic, and Bronze Age people in Denmark showed that the former ate a lot of food found in the sea. But over time there was a marked change: the younger Neolithic and Bronze Age communities became reliant on food from the land – even those that lived in coastal sites. By contrast, coastal communities in British Columbia have relied on marine resources consistently over millennia, although their children consumed less seafood and more land food than did the adults.

Nitrogen isotopes

Nitrogen (N) isotopes have also been found to reflect dietary preferences, with the proportion of N15 to N14 increasing up through the food chain from plant-dominated diets, as the intake of meat increases. For example, analysis of Neanderthal bones shows high ratios of N15 to N14, confirming that their diet was meat-based, as suspected from the archaeological evidence. Indeed, the isotope ratios are comparable to those found in the bones of active meat-eating predators such as wolves.

Strontium and calcium

Stable chemical elements such as strontium (Sr) and calcium (Ca) also provide evidence of diet. Generally plants take up traces of the two elements in proportion to their relative abundance in the soil and groundwater where they grow. However, the digestive systems of animals eating the plants preferentially take up whatever strontium is present in the plant matter. Most of the strontium is then excreted, but some traces are absorbed and "locked" into the mineral matter of the bones.

If the Sr/Ca ratio of the local environment is known, the importance of plants in the diet of any animal living in the area can assessed. For instance, Sr/Ca analysis of bone from *Australopithecus robustus* has shown that this massive-jawed extinct human was not purely vegetarian as previously thought. There is also the possibility of assessing whether the animal (or human relative) lived in the area for a significant time. Ötzi, the Neolithic so-called Ice Man of the Tyrol provides a good example of this kind of analysis (see p. 32). The Sr/Ca ratios in his bones and teeth did not match those of the soils where he was found. A better fit was found with the soils of the Lower Vinschgau valley to the south, although he was probably born even further south. Overall, it is likely that he never roamed much more than 60 km (37 miles) from his birthplace.

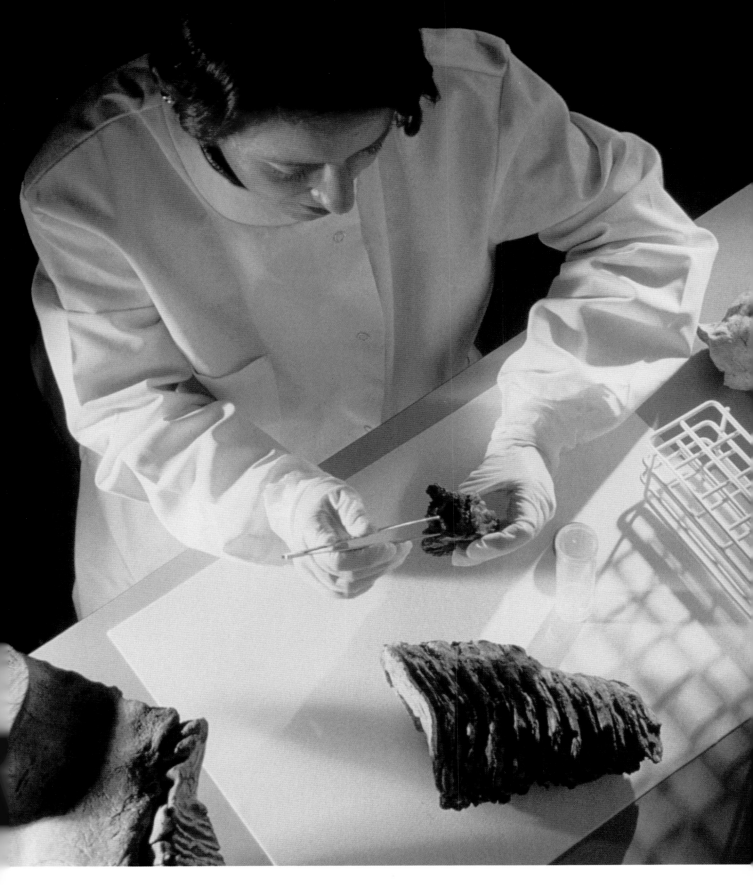

CONSTRUCTING A CALENDAR
Dating Techniques

An accurate chronological framework which allows artefacts, biological remains, and evidence for past events to be placed in their true historical context is essential for archaeology. That chronology has two elements: relative and absolute timing.

The study of the archaeology of the past few thousand years had the advantage that there was the possibility of recovering data that we could place within the known (and dated) calendars and chronologies of the historical record.

Early methods
But beyond this, in prehistoric time, we had to depend upon relative chronology based on superposition: older objects are found lower in a succession of archaeological deposits than younger ones, whether they are in a cave or on the seabed. There was also an expectation that cruder artefacts should be relatively older than more sophisticated ones, whether stone tools, pottery, or cave paintings. There was also a hope that similar artefacts could be used (biostratigraphically) like fossils of the same species to match deposits of similar age in otherwise geographically separated sites. The discovery of recognizable annual increments within some sediments such as lake-bed (varved) deposits and growth rings in tree wood held out the possibility of obtaining and extending some absolute dating into prehistory; however, while very useful and important, the application is quite limited.

The radioactivity revolution
These methods allowed huge advances in archaeology during the 19th and early 20th centuries, but there were still tremendous problems and gaps in understanding which could be resolved only by the development of new dating methods. The great breakthrough came from the discovery of radioactivity and the development of analytical techniques during World War II.

There are now a number of radiometric dating methods based on the principle that certain chemical elements have isotopes that decay at constant and measurable rates over time into "lighter" isotopes with lower atomic numbers. For instance, radiocarbon-14 has a half-life of 5730 years, over which half the C-14 in any sample decays into normal carbon-12. Because of this relatively short half-life, radiocarbon can only be used for dating materials less than 50,000 years old because beyond that so little C-14 is left. However, the arrival of accelerator mass spectroscopy (AMS) in the early 1980s allowed very small amounts of C-14 to be measured, so extending the technique back to around 80,000 years. Unfortunately, this method cannot be used for dating inorganic materials such as pottery or stone tools.

Dating of older materials, especially those relating to the evolution of extinct human (hominid) relatives who have existed over the past 7 million or so years, requires other radiometric methods such as potassium-argon and the uranium series. The problem with these is that they can only date the formation of certain minerals which mostly occur in volcanic rocks such as lavas and ashes. Luckily these are relatively abundant within the Great East African Rift Valley, where many of the most famous early hominid sites are found. It is important to realize that all these calculated radiometric dates bear a small percentage of error, despite being called "absolute dates". Many other dating techniques have been developed in recent years such as fission track, thermoluminescence, amino-acid racemization, and archaeomagnetic dating.

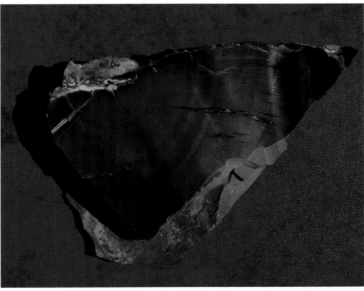

Top: A cross section of a modern tree, clearly showing the growth rings. These rings occur annually, thus creating one of the more basic dating techniques.

Above: A polished section of a petrified tree, photographed in Arizona. The growth rings can just be seen.

Above: A scientist cleaning a sample of a mammoth's tooth for dating using radiocarbon techniques.

FACING THE PAST
Facial Reconstruction

We humans recognize individuals by facial characters and even body "language", and often use the information to predict their thoughts and actions. With the current dominance of visual media and reconstruction of the past, there is a growing desire to know what our ancestors looked like.

Misrepresentations

For many years archaeologists have been considering the same question – with very mixed results. The extinct Neanderthal people have been consistently misrepresented from the late 19th century onwards, for example. Initially, interpretation of their skeletal remains led to their portrayal as dimwitted, club-wielding, brutal thugs, and even by the first decade of the 20th century French anthropologist Marcellin Boule saw them as stooped, bent-kneed, and round-shouldered individuals, a misinterpretation based on the severely arthritic Neanderthal skeleton from La Chapelle aux Saints.

Modern techniques

Until recently facial reconstruction was largely a matter of artistic inspiration, but it is now a much more exact technology, although the "breath of life" still requires the interpretive genius of the artist. A number of different disciplines from anatomy, plastic, and cosmetic surgery to computerized scanning tomography (CT scanning) and forensic science have contributed to the technology of modern facial and body reconstruction.

How do we reconstruct facial soft tissues which carry so many of our individual characteristics, along with features such as nose shape, hair, and eye colour, none of which is normally fossilized? Only mummification (by both natural and artificial means), especially by cold and sterile bogwater (for example, the Iron age Tollund man) or glacial ice (for example, Ötzi, the Neolithic hunter) preserves many individual facial characters.

Ever since World War II there have been dramatic developments in plastic surgery for victims of severe facial damage. Today, there are measures of the size and thickness of our unique multiplicity of facial muscles (even chimps have fewer) and skin tissues which can be built onto replica skulls to "flesh out" the basis of a face.

The main problems arise from the size and shape of the nose, ears, and lips, which leave little or no trace on the skull. If available, contemporary portraits of members of the same ethnic group can provide reliable guides to such details along with features such as hair style. Mummies present particular reconstruction problems because replication of the skull itself has, until recently, been impossible. But now non-destructive medical scanning techniques allow the 3D replication of skulls and can provide other vital information about medical conditions which might have affected the appearance of the individual.

Skulls

Often the skulls themselves are damaged, especially those of our more remote extinct ancestors, so the skull itself has to be reconstructed before anything else can be attempted. Palaeoanthropologists can spend months or years reconstructing some of their fossil skulls of ancient relatives such as *Kenyanthropus platyops*, reconstructed by Maeve Leakey. Even here, there is often a degree of subjectivity involved which can affect the final result, so that a small change in the slope of the face can make a reconstruction look more or less ape-like.

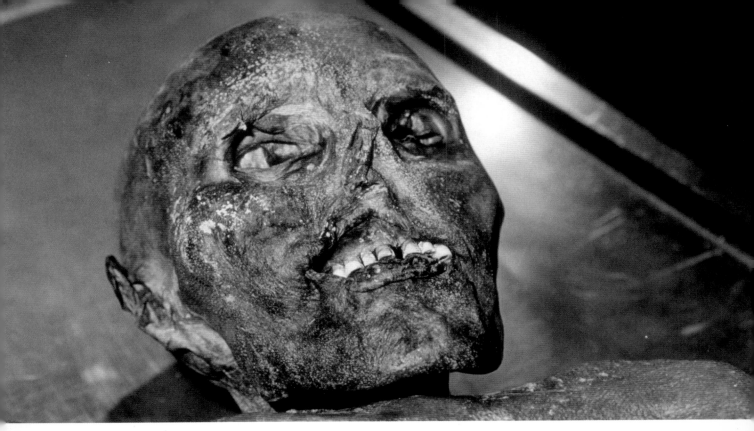

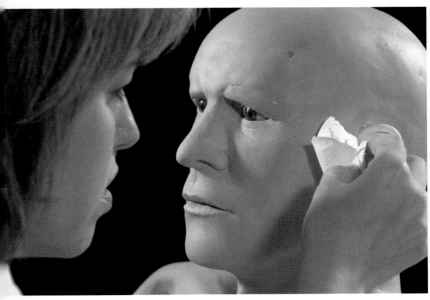

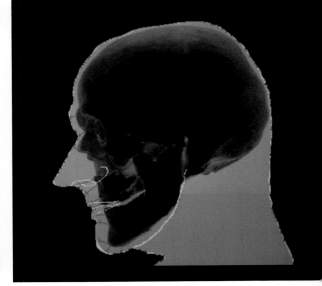

Top: Mummification, both natural and human induced, preserves some tissues but there is still shrinkage of fleshy structures such as the nose, ears, and lips, whose original form can be difficult to reconstruct.

Above: Facial reconstruction requires rebuilding of tissues such as the facial muscles along with skin, hair, and eyes. The dimensions and colour will vary according to ethnicity and individual variation.

Above: An x-ray of a head profile shows the extent to which the form of the human face is determined by the size and shape of the soft tissues, so accuracy depends upon supporting evidence such as a portrait or sculpture of a related individual.

FREEZES AND THAWS
Climate Modelling

For more than 150 years it has been evident that our ancestors lived through climate changes associated with a succession of Ice Ages over the past 2 million years. Initially, it was the sedimentary record and its fossil content of plants and animals which reflected changing environments and revealed extraordinary fluctuations in climate over the period.

At times ice sheets covered much of the British Isles and most of Canada, extending nearly as far south as today's London in England and Washington in the USA. Such glacial phases alternated with interglacials, when the climate was warmer than today and animals such as hippopotamuses and elephants lived around London. Such drastic changes must have impacted upon our prehistoric ancestors and extinct relatives (eg the *Homo erectus* and Neanderthal people). However, it is only recently and thanks to climate modelling that it has become possible to try to assess how they reacted to such environmental and climatic change and whether their evolution and extinction were affected in any way.

Indicators of change

The task of recovering accurate data about this history of climate change has been enormous. Most of the indicators of past climate change are indirect. There are numerous land-based sequences of sediment containing fossils such as plant pollen and insect remains which are climate-sensitive. But their dating and correlation over wide regions is often very difficult, and generally such sediment records span relatively short periods of time. However, recent decades have seen the recovery of much more extensive ice cores from polar regions (Greenland and Antarctica) and sediment cores from the deep oceans which provide detailed and often unbroken sequences of proxy data for climate change through the recent Ice Ages.

The indirect information on temperature change is derived from analysis of oxygen isotopes from air bubbles trapped in the ice cores and from the shells of abundant microfossils buried in ocean-floor sediments. Combined with increasingly accurate dating of the cores, it is now possible to establish rates of climate change, and these often turn out to have been remarkably rapid compared with the climates of the past 10,000 years, which were unusually stable. It is estimated that changes in average annual temperatures of as much as 5°C have occurred within 50 years or a single lifetime. Even with our modern technology a similar rate of change would be disastrous; the impact on our ancestors, their societies, and the environments within which they lived must have been even more problematic and at times catastrophic. By combining the chronology of proxy temperature records with sophisticated modern climate models (eg CLIMAP), based on modern understanding of ocean–atmosphere interactions, data about past ice distribution, and topography, a computer-generated framework of changing climate and environments can be constructed over time. The most abundant and best-quality data is at present confined to the past 100,000 years, covering the last interglacial and glacial for western Eurasia and North America. Climate change can be tracked at intervals as short as 5000 years, and so for the first time the archaeological record can be placed within a well-constrained framework of changing environments and climate.

Neanderthals and Cro-Magnons

Western Eurasia is particularly interesting in this context because the Neanderthals became extinct (around 28,000 years ago) during this interval and the Cro-Magnon (*Homo sapiens*) people invaded

the region, overlapping with the Neanderthals through some 10,000 years. The issue of whether the Neanderthals went "with a whimper or a bang", aided by either climate change or the Cro-Magnons, and whether they "interacted genetically" and left a genetic inheritance have been some of the big questions of recent human evolution.

So far it seems that both Neanderthals and modern "Cro-Magnon" humans had to retreat southwards in the face of deteriorating glacial conditions. With improving climate both groups could recolonize old abandoned territories, but the Cro-Magnons had a decided advantage. They had an expanding population base to the south

and east, while the Neanderthal population was probably much more finite. And the Cro-Magnons developed new technologies for superior clothing and tools which perhaps allowed them to exploit more marginal climatic territories, but ones which were nevertheless rich in game. Dwindling resources and fragmented populations made up of small groups meant that the Neanderthals, like much of the other megafauna of mammoth, woolly rhino, etc, could not recover from the maximum cold phase of the last Ice Age.

Above: A reconstruction showing some the browsers and big cats that could be found in London's Trafalgar Square during one of the interglacial periods.

INDEX

Page numbers in *italics* refer to captions and boxes. Those in **bold** refer to main entries